81 Mind-Blowing BIOLOGY FACTS

Every kid should know!

ARCTURUS

ARCTURUS
First edition published in 2024 by Arcturus Publishing Limited
26/27 Bickels Yard, 151–153 Bermondsey Street,
London SE1 3HA

Author: Anne Rooney
Illustrator: Nancy Butterworth
Consultant: Brett Baughman
Editor: Rebecca Razo
Designer: Stefan Holliland
Editorial Manager: Joe Harris

Published and Distributed in India by Scholastic India Pvt. Ltd.
First edition: 2024
This Reprint Edition: July 2024

ISBN: 978-93-5954-390-1
Printed in India at Shree Maitrey Printech Pvt. Ltd., Noida

Welcome to the Mind-Blowing World of Biology!

Did you know that plants can signal to each other if they're in danger of being eaten?

Or that the largest living thing in the world is a type of mushroom?

Or that snakes officially have four legs?

Biology is the study of living things, and every living thing on Earth is fair game for biologists. Some of those things are wild and wacky. This book is packed with amazing, jaw-dropping biology facts especially chosen to astound and fascinate you (and some just to make you giggle).

You'll find plenty to ponder and discuss, and you'll be able to impress people with your biology knowledge. Some of what you learn might even come in handy if, say, you hear a mosquito buzzing toward you or if you time-travel back to the world of dinosaurs.

There is no wrong way to use the book. You can start at the beginning and read straight through, or you can skip around and read whatever you find most interesting—the choice is yours! We've also included tons of illustrations. A few are matter-of-fact, but most are fun and quirky to entertain you while you learn.

Ready to have your mind blown by biology? Turn the page to get started!

1 Springtails really have a spring

A springtail is a little jointed animal that has six legs like an insect. Most springtails are less than 6 mm (0.24 in) long. They also have a nifty way of escaping danger—they can use a special folded organ under their body to launch themselves into the air at a moment's notice.

The spring isn't in the tail

The spring is called the "furcula," and it's attached under the fourth body segment. Most of the time, the furcula is folded under the body and held in place, under tension, by a band of tough tissue. When the springtail needs to make a speedy getaway, the furcula is released, and instantly slams down against the surface the animal is standing on, catapulting it into the air. The whole process takes less than 1/50th of a second.

Animals cannot grow wheels

A spring is fine, but it's impossible for an animal to evolve wheels. To spin freely, a wheel needs to move around on its axle without being connected to it. Without a connection to its "wheel," the animal couldn't supply blood to it or link it into its nervous system. That would make it impossible to grow the wheel in the first place!

DID YOU KNOW?

A type of springtail is the only animal that naturally lives all the time on the mainland of Antarctica.

2 Mushrooms aren't plants

Most people think of mushrooms as plants, but they're not. They often grow on the ground like plants and they take their nourishment from the surface they grow on. Also, they don't move around or make noise. Although they share these similarities with plants, biologists classify mushrooms as fungi—a group entirely separate from both plants and animals.

In the kingdom of the mushroom

Along with the mushrooms you might eat, fungi include toadstools and tiny organisms like some yeast—some can even grow on your body, causing conditions like athlete's foot. Fungi don't produce seeds. They reproduce (make more of themselves) by making spores. Unlike seeds, spores don't contain a food source for the new growing organism. The spores must land somewhere with the necessary nutrients if the organism is to survive.

Domains and kingdoms

Science divides all living things into three "domains" and then divides the domains into "kingdoms." These are further divided into smaller categories until each organism (living thing) has its own species.

The three domains are eukaryotes, bacteria, and archaea. Everything with more than one cell, from a mushroom to a whale, belongs to the eukaryote domain. Eukaryotes are divided into several kingdoms, including plants, animals, and fungi. Bacteria and archaea are both tiny organisms with one cell, although the structure of the cells is different because they evolved separately.

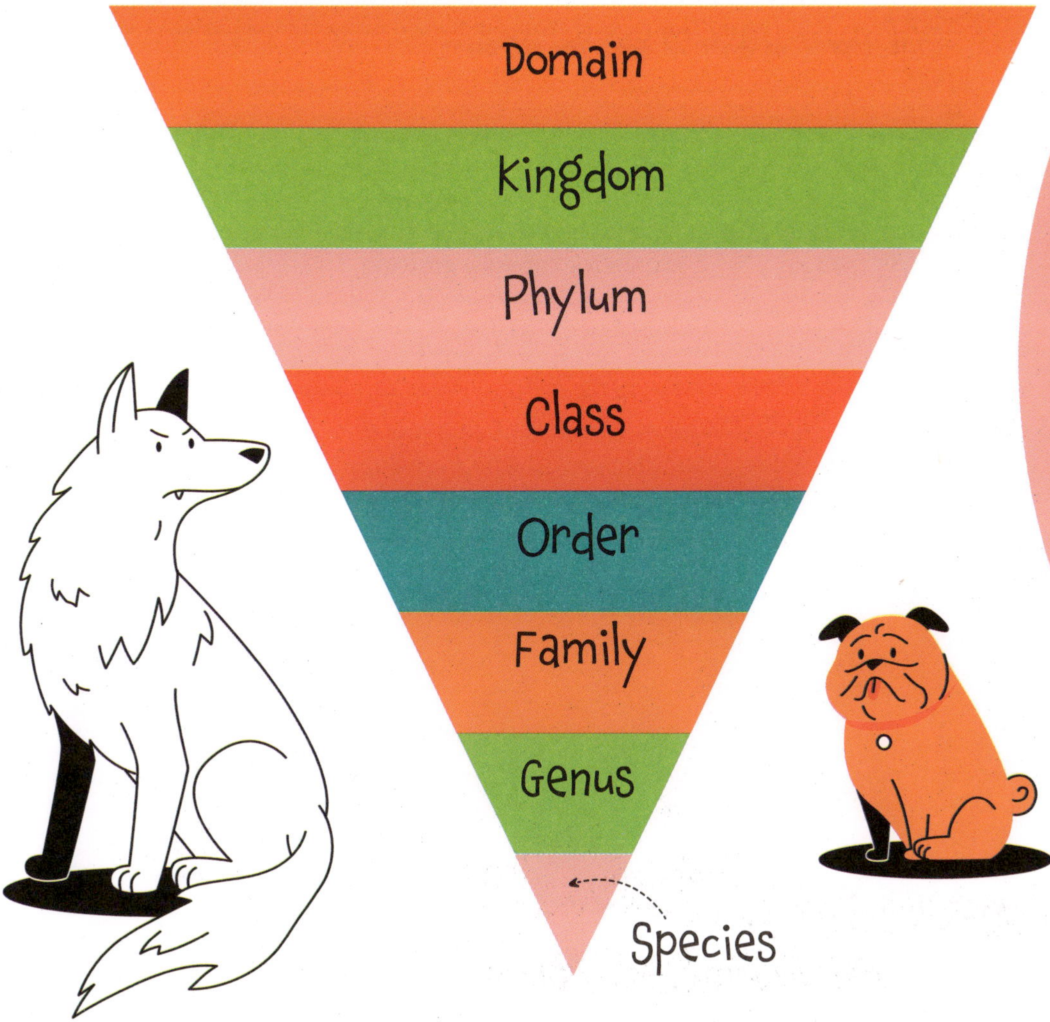

3 *Stegosaurus* and *T. rex* never met

The first dinosaurs appeared about 240 million years ago. They survived for around 175 million years before their sudden extinction (dying out) 66 million years ago—although no single type of dinosaur lived for all of those years. Many of the most well-known dinosaurs, such as *Stegosaurus* and *T. rex,* never met each other because they lived at different times or in different places.

Starting out

The first dinosaurs weren't giants at all. Most were nimble and quite slender, good at running away from larger, fiercer reptiles. The dinos moved up in the world about 200 million years ago when many of their competitors died out. The Jurassic period (201–145 million years ago) was the heyday of the giants like *Diplodocus* and *Brontosaurus.* It also saw famous dinos such as *Stegosaurus* and *Allosaurus.* Other famed dinosaurs, such as *T. rex, Triceratops,* and *Parasaurolophus* lived toward the end of the Cretaceous (145–66 million years ago.) Some would have been around to see an asteroid plunge into the coast of Mexico—and wipe them all out.

Here and now, or there and then?

T. rex lived 80 million years after *Stegosaurus,* while you live only 66 million years after *T. rex*. That means *T. rex* could have found *Stegosaurus* fossils if it had gone looking (though those tiny arms wouldn't have been good for digging!). Other dinosaurs would never have met because they lived too far apart. We can be sure that no *Parasaurolophus,* which lived in North America, was ever bitten by a *Velociraptor,* which lived in Mongolia.

4 Bowerbirds like blue

Male satin bowerbirds collect lots of blue things to make their nests look pretty. They do this to attract a mate. The bird with the best collection of blue things is most likely to win the best female!

Wooing ways

Among birds and some other animals, it's often the female that chooses a mate. Males try to impress the females so that they are chosen. Many male birds build an appealing nest or collect objects to attract a female. Others just have very pretty plumage (feathers), sing a beautiful song, or even do a special type of dance to attract attention.

Building a bower

The bowerbird's bower is a place where the male bird displays the objects he's collected and waits for admiring females to inspect them. He might gather blue plastic bottle tops, blue glass, blue flowers, blue berries, blue feathers from other birds, and any other blue items lying around. Some have been said to paint things blue if they don't have enough blue things! They do this by mashing up blue berries with their beaks and smearing the pulp on objects.

Not a nest

The bower is a structure made of sticks and its only purpose is to attract a mate. Females inspect all the bowers and later watch the males perform a dance. The female chooses a male that performs well and has an impressive collection of objects. The female makes a separate uncluttered nest to lay eggs and raise her chicks.

5 The largest living thing is a mushroom

The largest organism on Earth isn't a blue whale or a giant tree—it's a type of honey mushroom found in the state of Oregon, USA. The giant fungus spreads underground over an area of nearly 10 sq km (4 sq mi).

Tip of the iceberg

The mushrooms and toadstools you might see growing in a garden or woodland are just the top visible part of a much larger organism. Most of the fungus consists of a network of threads that run under the soil or through rotting wood, stretching for incredibly long distances. The visible part is the fruiting body—the bit the fungus sends up to release the spores that it uses to reproduce. As the fruiting body ripens, it opens up and the wind carries the spores away to start another giant fungus somewhere else.

Keep on growing

The record-breaking fungus in Oregon has been there a long time. Scientists say it's probably 2,400 years old and could even be as old as 8,650 years. That means it started growing before the Roman Empire began, possibly before the Ancient Egyptians existed, and maybe even while there were still woolly mammoths roaming the Earth!

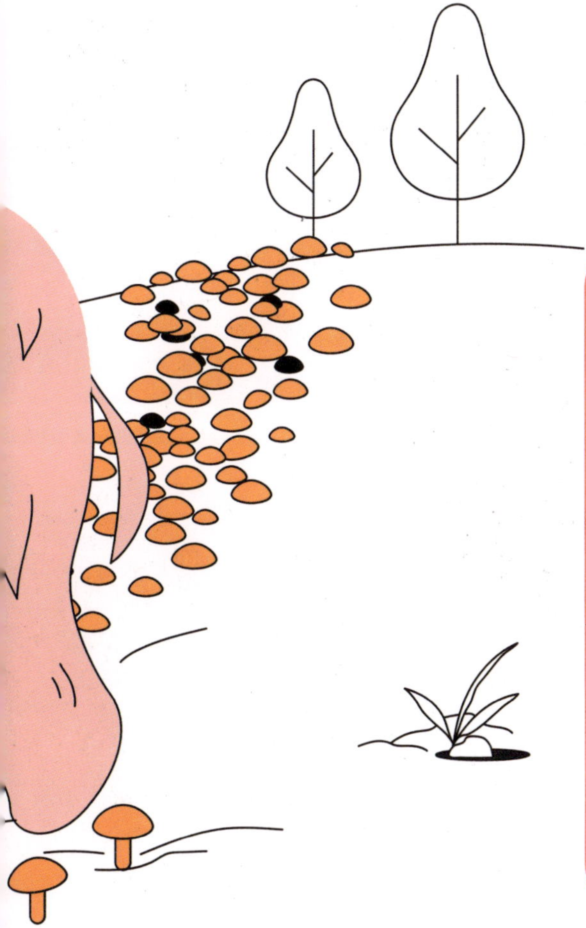

6 Some mushrooms are deadly

The most poisonous fungus is the death cap mushroom, which grows in much of the world. It looks harmless—it even looks like some mushrooms that are edible—which makes it extra dangerous. Just half a mushroom contains enough poison to kill a human, and cooking it doesn't kill the poison! So, don't ever pick a mushroom in the wild and eat it!

7 Aphids can produce more babies in a year than there are people on Earth

Aphids, or greenflies, are tiny insects that live on plants, feeding on the sap (juice) from the stem and leaves. They're odd in that they can clone themselves—female aphids can give birth to baby aphids without needing to mate with a male.

New aphids are born already pregnant with more clones! They mature quickly and a single aphid could, in theory, produce hundreds of millions more aphids in just one summer. They could make a line of aphids nearly 200,000 km (more than 120,000 mi) long!

The more the merrier

By cloning themselves, aphids can quickly colonize a plant and spread to others. They don't need to wait around for a father to help them produce young. Every new aphid clone is exactly the same as its mother—and they're all female. Of course, not every new aphid survives to produce more, or the world would disappear under a thick blanket of aphids in no time. Many are eaten by other animals, including birds, reptiles, and other insects.

Cloning is bad for you

Making a clone is a type of asexual reproduction (reproducing without a partner organism). It's not ideal, because it means there's no chance to mix and match features, which helps organisms adapt to changing circumstances. But late in the summer, some males are born. They mate with females, which then lay eggs. The eggs overwinter (live through winter) to ensure there will be more aphids the following summer to start the process all over again.

8 Some mammals lay eggs

You've probably heard that one of the features that defines a mammal is that it gives birth to live young (babies). Birds, amphibians (like frogs), reptiles (like crocodiles), and many fish lay eggs. But there are a few mammals that lay eggs, too. They're called "monotremes." All five types live in Australia or New Guinea.

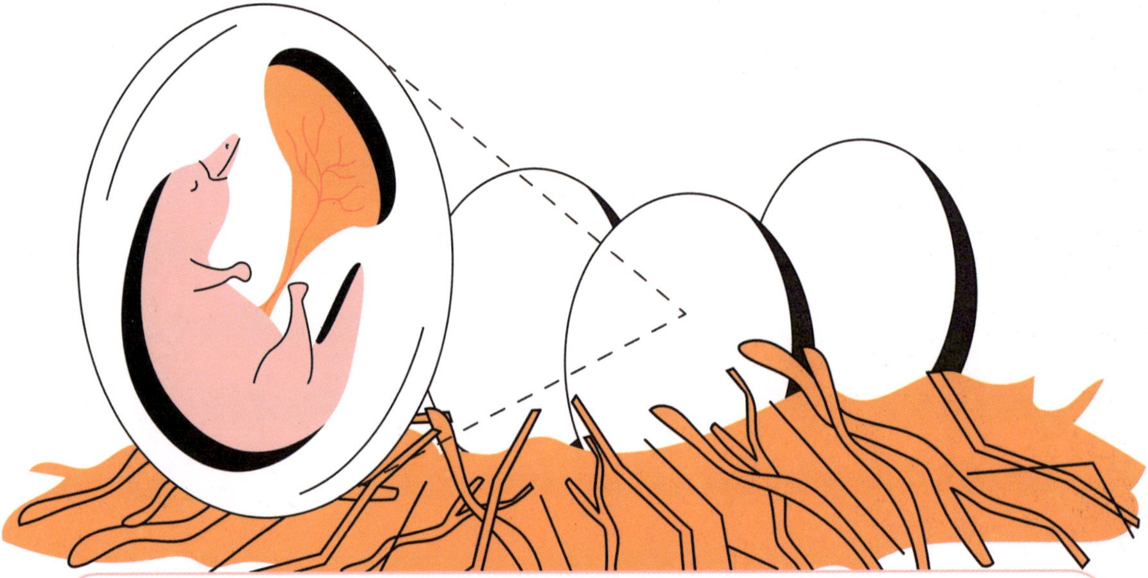

Safe inside

Most mammals grow their babies from an egg that stays inside the mother's body. The egg is very tiny, and it grows in a part of the mother's body called the uterus (womb). A new organ, called the "placenta," grows. The placenta links the mother to the embryo (that will grow into a baby), providing all that the embryo needs to grow and develop. By growing her babies inside her body, a female mammal keeps them safe. An egg developing in a nest is in danger of being eaten, lost, trodden on, or getting too hot or cold. Inside a mother, the growing baby is protected by her body and is generally safe as long as the mother is safe.

Being different

Monotremes hark back to the ancestors of all mammals. Mammals evolved more than 200 million years ago and the earliest examples laid eggs, just like the reptile-like animals that came before them. Today, there are five types of monotremes: the duck-billed platypus and four types of echidna. They find their food using electrolocation, which means they pick up the electric field produced by living things.

9 Babies have more bones than adults

Human babies are born with extra bits of bone. As the baby grows, some bones fuse together and so the total number of bones in their body reduces. Babies have around 270 bones, but by the time they're adults they have only 206–213 bones.

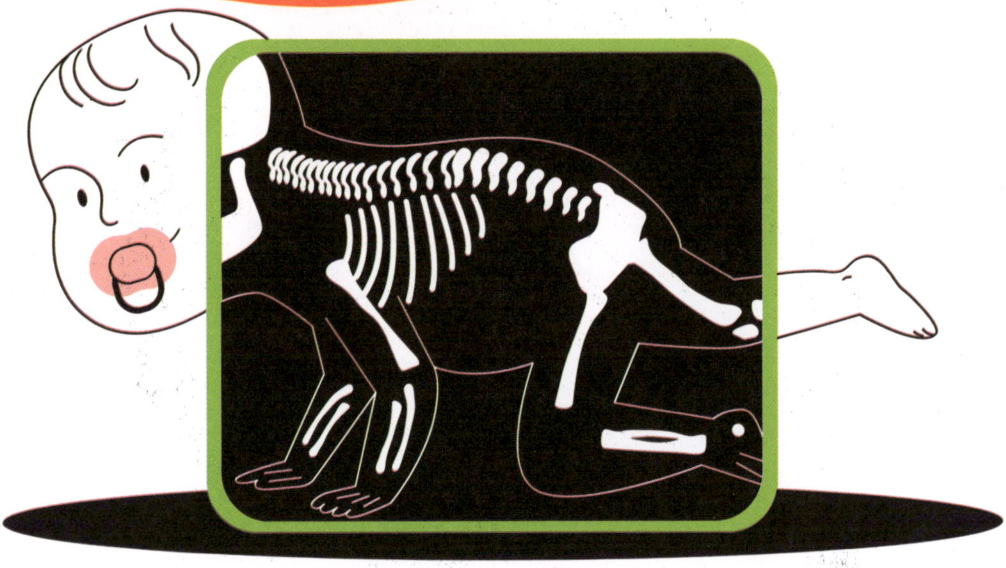

Bone and cartilage

Bone is a hard and brittle substance, while cartilage, though tough, is more flexible. Much of a baby's skeleton is made of cartilage to start with, but it turns to bone as the child grows. Cartilage starts changing to bone before birth, but the process isn't complete until a person is in their twenties. Because cartilage is not as brittle as bone, children can often take tumbles and accidents that would break an adult's bones. (It's still important to be careful!)

Ears and nose

Some cartilage never changes to bone. The hard parts of your nose and ears stay cartilage for your whole life.

DID YOU KNOW?

Some animals have skeletons that are made entirely of cartilage. Dogfish are an example.

10 Babies are born with holes in their heads

A newborn baby has gaps in the skull called "fontanelles." These make soft spots on the head. The fontanelles slowly close as bone grows across them. The gaps are useful because they allow for the growth of the brain and skull during the baby´s first year.

11 On average, your heart will beat two billion times in your life

Most adults have a resting heart rate of 60–70 beats per minute. A person who lives to be 70 years old will have two billion heartbeats altogether. The longer a person lives, the more heartbeats they will have.

Take it easy-ish

On average, people who live longest have a lower resting heart rate. Your resting heart rate is how quickly your heart beats when you've been inactive for a while. Lots of things can upset that average, including illness and genetics. Stress can raise your heart rate, so staying chilled is a good idea. But exercise raises your heart rate, too, and that's good for you, so it's not all about being totally laid back.

Pumping blood

Your heart "beats" because it's a muscle that contracts (squeezes itself) to pump blood around your body. Blood carries oxygen to the tissues of your body, including your muscles. The more the muscles move, the more oxygen they need so your heart beats faster when you're active to send more oxygen to the muscles that help you run, swim, or cycle.

Fast and furious

Other animals have different heart rates and lifespans. A hamster's heart beats 450 times a minute, but a hamster lives only about three years. It can still fit in nearly a billion heartbeats. A whale's heart beats only 20 times a minute, but it doesn't live much longer than a human, so it manages about a billion heartbeats, too.

12 Honey never goes bad

With most food in your cupboard, you need to check to make sure it's not too old before you eat it, but honey is almost always safe as long as the jar is unopened. Even jars of honey that were buried with ancient Egyptian pharaohs thousands of years ago haven't gone bad!

Sticky, but dry

Honey is a thick, sticky liquid that contains almost no water. That's one of the secrets of its everlasting shelf life. For a food to spoil, microbes need to be able to grow in it. Because there's so little water in honey, even microbes that don't need air can't survive.

A bee's tummy kills microbes

Bees make honey. It begins as nectar that bees collect from flowers and eat (see page 44). A bee's stomach produces a chemical (enzyme) that breaks down the nectar, which begins the honey-making process. One of the products of the digestion is hydrogen peroxide, which kills microbes.

Because microbes can't grow in honey, it is also useful in medicine. It has been spread on wounds and skin conditions for thousands of years to help them heal. The honey pulls water from the wound and then makes an air-tight barrier that microbes can't cross. The tiny amount of hydrogen peroxide in the honey even helps healing.

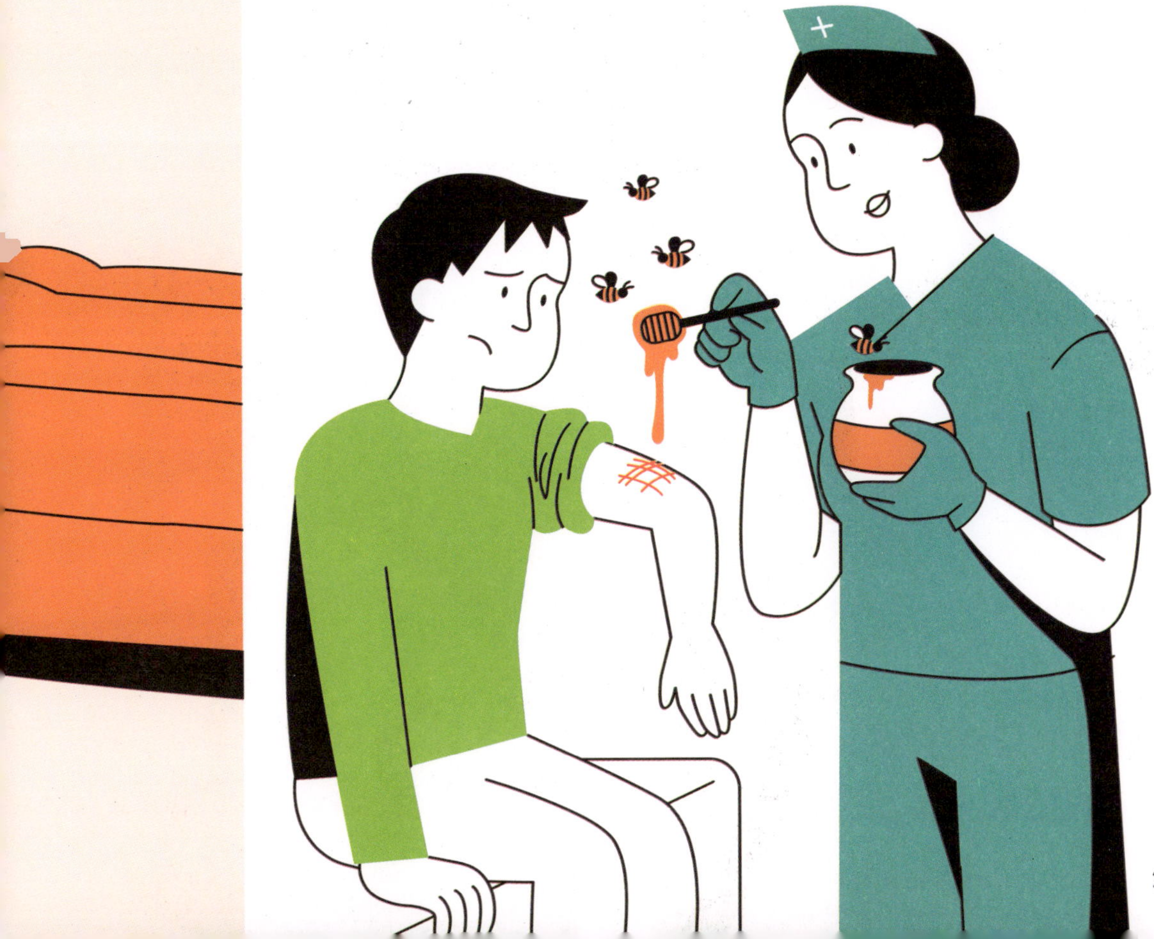

13 Snails can sleep for three years

You would think a snail doesn't need much sleep since it doesn't do a whole lot during the day. But it has regular awake and asleep times—like you—and it can also sleep for much longer if conditions aren't snail friendly.

A snail's day

A snail normally sleeps for about 15 hours and then is active for around 30 hours. This means it's not working on a normal day–night cycle as we do. A snail's single sleep-wake cycle is about the equivalent of two human days.

Too dry, too cold

Snails need moisture so that they can produce the slime they need to move forward. That's why you see them more often after it's rained than when it's dry. If it's dry or cold, they tend to stay safely in their shell. And if it's cold or dry for a very long time—even up to three years—they stay inside and wait for conditions to improve.

Why sleep?

When we're asleep, our bodies carry out essential repairs. That's why you sleep more when you're ill or injured. The right amount of sleep is important for mental and physical health. If a person is never allowed to sleep, they will eventually die. But scientists still know relatively little about how sleep works, especially in animals. They don't know whether all animals sleep, or whether, say, tadpoles or worms don't need to sleep. Some animals, including dolphins and whales, sleep with half their brain at a time so that they're always alert enough to spot danger—and to rise to the surface to breathe.

14 A giant tree is made mostly of water and air

Trees grow in soil, but they use very little of it. Most of a tree is made from chemicals it has taken from air and water, not from soil. This was demonstrated in the 1630s by a Belgian scientist, Jan Baptist van Helmont.

Do plants eat soil?

Until van Helmont carried out his experiment, people believed that plants "ate" soil in order to grow. He showed that plants actually have a very small appetite for soil. He weighed a small willow sapling and a pot full of dry soil. Then he planted the tree in the soil, covered the pot so that nothing could fall into the soil, and looked after it carefully for five years, watering it and keeping it in sunlight. At the end of five years, he dried the soil and weighed the tree and soil again. He found the tree had increased in weight by 75 kg (165 lbs), but the weight of the soil had dropped by only 57 g (2 oz). He concluded the whole tree was made almost entirely from water—but he was wrong.

Plants need sunlight

As well as water, plants need sunlight and carbon dioxide, which is a gas they take from the air. Plants, including van Helmont's tree, use the energy of sunlight to power a reaction between water and carbon dioxide. The result is the sugar glucose, which the plant uses to fuel its growth, and the gas oxygen, which the plant releases into the air—and which humans and all other animals breathe.

15 Giant fungi once grew 6 m (20 ft) tall

Around 420–350 million years ago, a giant fungus grew as a single column straight up from the ground. Called Prototaxites, its trunk was around 1 m (3.3 ft) across, and it grew as tall as a large giraffe.

Biggest on the land

At the time Prototaxites was growing, there were no large animals with backbones living on land—just millipedes, worms, and wingless insects. All plants were very simple and small. Prototaxites would have towered over everything else.

16 A teaspoon of soil can contain miles of fungi strands

Many fungi live underground, growing as long, thin filaments (threads). These are so thin that the filaments in a single teaspoonful of soil, laid end to end, would stretch for many miles.

Forest network

Fungal threads weave through all the soil of a forest floor and connect with the tips of tree roots. Trees use the fungal "network" to communicate with each other and share nutrients (chemicals used as food). The fungi take about a third of the sugars that the trees make from photosynthesis—it's their "fee" for transporting chemicals between trees! Through the network of fungi, trees send nourishment to saplings that are not tall enough to get much light and support trees that are sick or dying. At the heart of the networks are hub or "mother" trees that communicate with and support many others. The trees and fungus both win from the arrangement, and a healthy forest is one well populated with trees, other plants, and fungi.

17 Snakes officially have four legs...

...at least they are classed as quadrupeds, which means "four-footed." Snakes are reptiles, and reptiles originally evolved as four-footed animals that lived on land. They evolved from amphibians, which also have four feet. At some point in their 150-million-year history, snakes lost their legs and ended up slithering over the ground.

From four to two

Snakes lost their legs when they started to live in burrows. Obviously, if you want to slither into a small hole, legs can be a nuisance. Snake fossils from the Cretaceous period 145-66 million years ago show snakes with two stubby legs, so they seem to have lost one pair of legs and then the other.

A bit left

Some modern snakes, including boa constrictors and pythons, have left-over bits of hip and thigh bones. They don't have legs anymore, but the last bits of bone for legs and attaching legs still remain hidden inside the snake.

Not needed

Just as evolution helps organisms to develop structures that are useful, it helps them to lose those that are not useful. If having legs doesn't give an animal any advantages, those born without legs will be at least as successful, so this "leglessness" will increase. Having legs one doesn't need wastes energy and tissue on growth and might even lead to injury or harm. Snakes without legs have taken over from snakes with useless legs.

18 Whales once lived on land

Whales are mammals, so they need to breathe air. They evolved from land-going animals that initially looked a bit like dogs and which gradually adapted to life in the water.

Land whales

Whales, dolphins, and porpoises are classed as "cetaceans," a special type of sea-going mammal. The earliest known cetacean was an animal about 1 m (3.3 ft) long that looked like a wolf with a very long head. Called *Pakicetus,* it lived 50 million years ago on land that is now part of Pakistan. It ate meat and fish, catching the fish by swimming in the shallow ocean it lived beside. The long skull of *Pakicetus* is still a feature of modern cetaceans.

Getting wet

As *Pakicetus* hunted fish, it became better adapted to living in the water. Over millions of years, its descendants turned their legs to flippers and their long wolf-tail to a strong, thick tail for swimming. The front legs became strong flippers, but eventually the back legs disappeared entirely.

19 Whales count as hoofed animals

Cetaceans evolved on land. They had hoofed feet and ankle bones similar to those of other hoofed animals, such as horses. Although they have lost their legs, some whales still have tiny remnants of leg bones hidden within their bodies. The gray whale is an example.

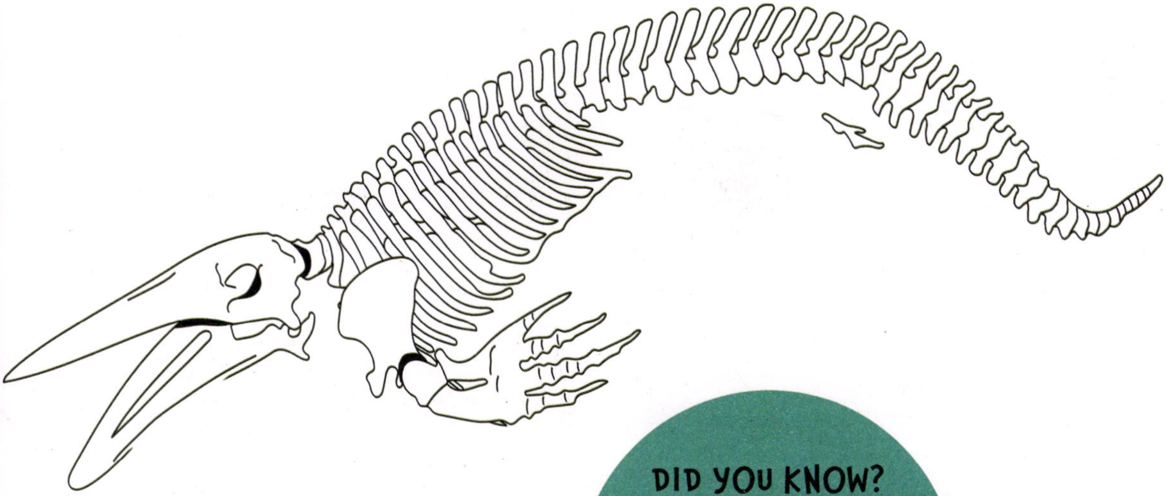

DID YOU KNOW?

Toothed whales have only one nostril called a "blowhole." It's on top of their head and is the hole they blow water from when they surface.

20 We can put a plant to sleep

General anesthetics are used in medicine to put a patient to sleep before an operation. Scientists have found that they affect plants, too. An anesthetic applied to a plant's roots stops the electrical waves that move through the plant. In animals, nerves carry messages around the body using electricity.

Moving plants

Most plants stay still and just grow, but a few actually move. A plant called mimosa, or "sensitive plant," curls its leaves up when they're touched. But giving the plant an anesthetic stops it doing this. The anesthetic works on the plant in the same way as it would on an animal. Does this mean plants are conscious, like animals, in some way? Scientists are trying to find out.

21 Plants recognize their relatives...

... and they're nice to them! Plants grown alongside others they're related to grow differently from those grown next to plants that are "strangers." They appear to share sunlight with relatives, but not with strangers.

Sharing sunlight

Plants usually compete for sunlight, as it's a resource they need to survive. Experimenters have found that some plants grown in rows with their relatives grew fewer leaves on the sides where their relations needed sunlight than on the sides where there was no plant. But they weren't as considerate if grown in a row of unrelated plants. It seems the plants are detecting light reflected from the leaves of those growing next to them and adjusting their growth if they recognize the leaf pattern of a relative!

22 Some dinosaurs grew to 10,000 times their size at hatching

Giant dinosaurs like *Diplodocus* and *Brontosaurus* had tiny babies. They had to grow quickly to reach their huge adult size.

Limits on eggs

Some dinosaurs laid long, thin eggs, but sauropods laid eggs that were nearly spherical. Even though the adult dinosaurs could grow to 27 m (90 ft), the babies had to fit into an egg the size of a grapefruit, only 26 cm across (10 in). Having spherical eggs allowed for as much space inside as possible for growth, but it still wasn't much space for a creature that would grow so large. You'd think the dinosaurs could just lay bigger eggs, but there seems to be a limit to the size an egg can be. A large egg needs a thick shell to protect it from breaking, but large eggs with thick shells are demanding on the mother's body and are too hard for the baby to crack open when it's time to emerge.

23 An egg is a single cell

The body of every living organism is made up of cells. An adult human has more than 30 trillion cells, while a microbe typically has only one cell. Most cells are tiny but some are very big. All animal eggs—from insects to birds and even crocodiles—are a single cell. The largest is an ostrich egg, which can measure 15 cm (6 in) long!

24 A high-pitched mosquito might bite you

Only female mosquitoes bite because they're the only ones that feed on blood. They do this because they need protein from us to make their eggs. Male mosquitoes feed only on nectar from flowers. Fortunately for us, mosquitoes make a distinctive whining sound that warns us when they're around; however, males and females whine in different tones. On the musical scale, female mosquitoes whine around upper F and males whine around upper C.

Beating wings

Mosquitoes flap their wings extremely fast: 350–500 beats per second for females and 450–700 beats per second for males. Scientists measure frequency in Hertz (Hz). Mosquito wing-beat frequency, called its "flight tone," is 575 Hz for males and 450 Hz for females. It's the beating wings that make the whining sound, so they only make noise while flying. They don't make noise while biting you—or while they're resting and thinking about biting you.

Mosquito talk

Mosquitoes can change the pitch of their flight zone by changing the speed at which they flap their wings. They do this when they meet another mosquito to check out their new companion. If it's a boy–girl match, that's great, and the pair continue to buzz in harmony. If it's not, they change their sound again and look for another mosquito.

Whine and dine

You're more likely to hear a female mosquito whine than a male, as the females are attracted to your body and males aren't. If they can smell your tasty blood, they'll come around and you'll be able to hear them. Males make as much noise, but they're not interested in eating you for lunch.

25 You can kill a plant with petroleum jelly

Petroleum jelly is an oily substance that water can't pass through. You might have used it to prevent your lips from drying out in the cold, which happens when water evaporates from your lips. But a plant wouldn't choose to use petroleum jelly. If you stop a plant losing water, it won't live long.

Necessary holes

Smearing petroleum jelly on the underneath of a plant's leaves stops the flow of water through the plant. Plants have holes called "stomata" on the undersides of their leaves. These holes are used in transpiration, which is the plant's way of losing water to the air. Plants take water in from the soil through their roots; the water then travels up the stem to the leaves, where it's lost to the air through evaporation from the stomata. Water carries necessary chemicals around the plant. Blocking the stomata stops the flow and prevents the plant from pulling water up from the roots.

Taking control

A plant controls its flow of water by opening and closing its stomata. On a hot day, in dry soil, the plant closes its stomata so that water isn't pulled too quickly out of its leaves. Opening all the stomata would make the plant dry out if there wasn't enough water in the soil to keep the flow going. If the plant has plenty of water it can open the stomata and let the water flow, carrying the chemicals it needs to grow. In summer, with bright sunlight to provide energy and enough rain, plants grow well—as long as there is no petroleum jelly on their leaves!

26 Fish have no neck

An important difference between you and a fish is how you can move your head. All tetrapods (animals with four legs) have a neck that allows them to move their head from side to side and up and down, but a fish can't do that.

Limited movement

A fish can't turn its head to the side. If it wants to face to the left or right, it has to turn its whole body. It can move its head up and down a little, just as much as it needs in order to feed, but it's all or nothing for fish movement—either the whole body turns or none of it turns.

Head to shoulders

Your head is separated from your shoulders by your neck. But a fish's shoulders are attached straight to its skull! You might think a fish doesn't need shoulders because it has no arms; however, fish have fins at the front that attach to the "pectoral girdle" (a scientific term for shoulders in both fish and people). With a neck, you can twist, lower, and raise your head without moving your shoulders. For a fish, moving the head means moving parts of the backbone (vertebrae) beyond the shoulders. So, when the head goes up and down, so do the fins.

27 Honey is technically bee "vomit"—ewww!

Bees make honey as a way to feed themselves and their young in the winter. They make the honey in their stomach and then spit it back up to store in the honeycomb for future use.

DID YOU KNOW?

It takes 12 honeybees their whole lives to make a single teaspoon of honey.

Sickly sweet, sweetly sick

Bees collect nectar from flowers using long tongues that work like straws. A bee's tongue is hollow, so it can suck up nectar, which it then stores in a special internal pouch called a "honey stomach." When a bee is full, it returns to the hive where it passes the nectar back out of its mouth into the mouths of other bees (yuck!), who then chew it up for about 30 minutes and pass it on to other bees. It goes around the bees until it is ready to be made into honey. The bees "spit" the liquid into little hexagonal cells other bees have made. Then they fan their wings over it to create a draft, making any extra water evaporate. This turns the substance from liquid to thick, sticky goo, which we use as honey.

28 Bees can see things you can't

You can see light in the range from red to violet, but bees can also see ultraviolet light, which is off the end of the scale for humans. Many flowers have patterns called "nectar guides" that direct honeybees to where the flower has its nectar. Sometimes you can see these, but others only show up in ultraviolet light, which only the bees can see.

29 Some dolphins and whales are born hairy...

... and so are some human babies. Both are hairy in the womb, before they're born. The hair, which falls out just before or soon after birth, is called "lanugo."

Hairy mammals

Vertebrates (animals with a backbone) can be mammals, birds, reptiles, amphibians, or fish. Each group has some special characteristics that help us identify them. Almost all mammals give birth to live babies, and all female mammals produce milk from their bodies to feed their babies. Mammals also have hair—even if it's only a few whiskers. Many are completely covered with hair. Both humans and cetaceans (whales and dolphins) evolved from fully hairy mammals.

30 Some mammals keep their babies in a pocket

Mammals called "marsupials" give birth to very small, underdeveloped babies. These crawl over the mother's fur and into a pouch—a sort of pocket on the front of her body. There they drink her milk and grow bigger—developing in the pouch like other mammals that develop inside their mother's body in the womb. Kangaroos and koalas are marsupials.

From outside to inside

Millions of years ago, the ancestors of all mammals laid eggs. That changed about 60 million years ago, with some mammals keeping their eggs inside their bodies. The stage at which the baby is born varies. Some animals are born fully functional while others are completely helpless. A baby gazelle can stand and run within minutes of being born, but a human baby can only suck milk. Marsupial babies are not only helpless—they're half-developed. They can't survive outside the pouch until they've done some growing.

31 One whale equals 20 trees

To fight climate change, we need to cut the amount of carbon dioxide in the air. One way to accomplish this is to plant trees, which take in carbon and lock it away in their wood. But whales also lock away carbon. Over its lifetime, a whale locks away as much carbon as about 20 trees—and keeps it locked away for longer than a tree.

Grow a tree or a whale?

A tree takes in carbon dioxide and splits it into oxygen and carbon as it photosynthesizes (see page 27). It releases the oxygen back into the air and makes sugar using the carbon. This is a building block for other chemicals. Much of the carbon stays in the tree and is slowly released when the tree dies and the wood rots.

A blue whale doesn't photosynthesize, but it eats tiny phytoplankton that do. They lock away carbon, and their carbon becomes part of the whale that eats them. Whales live a long time, and when they die, they usually sink to the seabed. It can take more than 100 years for a dead whale to decompose and release the carbon.

How many whales?

More whales means more phytoplankton, as the chemicals in waste from whales helps phytoplankton to grow. And more phytoplankton means more whales. Even a one-percent increase in phytoplankton locks away as much carbon as 2 billion trees. The world has room for a lot more whales. There were once more than 30 times as many blue whales as there are now. Bring back the whales!

32 There is human poop on the Moon

Twelve astronauts visited the Moon between 1969 and 1972. They needed to make their rocket as light as possible for the return journey so they left all their tools and their waste behind—including several bags containing poop, vomit, and food waste. About half of human poop is bacteria—It contains more than 1,000 species of different microbes. No one knows what might have happened to those microbes on the Moon.

Poor living conditions

Many scientists think it unlikely any microbes are still alive in those bags of waste left on the Moon, but it would be good to check. The Moon doesn't have nice living conditions for organisms. There is no air, and the temperature swings between extremely cold at -173 °C (-280 °F) and extremely hot at 100 °C (212 °F). With no atmosphere, the Moon is bombarded by cosmic rays and ultraviolet radiation from the Sun. It would be hard for microbes to live there.

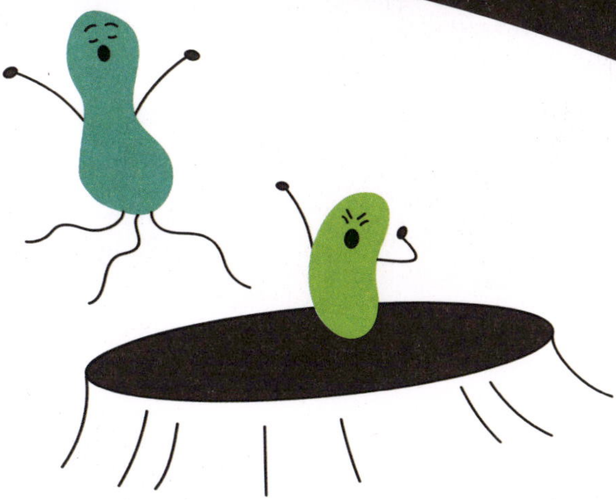

Growing or dying?

If scientists find that there *are* living microbes in the human waste on the Moon, that tells us important things about how life might survive in places other than Earth. If things can live in such extreme temperatures, bombarded by radiation and with no air, who knows where we might find life in space? If microbes have survived on the Moon for more than 50 years, that suggests they might be able to travel through space on asteroids (space rocks) and maybe move between planets to start new lives somewhere else.

33 Nearly half of Earth's microbes live deep underground

We think of Earth's surface as teeming with life, but in fact there's almost as much life far beneath our feet. Around 45 percent of all the microbes on Earth live deep in the rocks. It's the largest habitat on Earth.

Eating chemicals

Microbes that live deep in the rocks can't depend on oxygen from the air or on heat from the Sun to survive. Instead, they use chemicals called hydrocarbons (made mostly of hydrogen and carbon) and use the heat that comes from inside Earth. They live several miles below the surface and feed on chemicals like petroleum (crude oil). Scientists have found them when scooping mud from places where petroleum has leaked into the sea from the rocks.

Long, long lives

Petroleum-eating microbes don't like to live in seawater at a normal temperature, but they can survive as spores, becoming active again if they end up somewhere hot enough. They can survive for thousands, or even millions, of years as spores, and start up again if they reach another underground petroleum deposit. They're the most resilient life forms known.

34 Cold-loving bacteria live beneath the ice of Antarctica

Not all microbes like heat. Some live deep under the ice sheet of Antarctica.

Here they feed on rocks—or chemicals that have come from rocks and are dissolved in the water—and on the decaying bodies of other microbes. The existence of these microbes leads scientists to wonder whether there could be microbes living under the ice of other planets and their moons.

35 Humans account for 1/10,000th of the biomass of living things

People make up only 0.01 percent of the biomass of living things on Earth. There's about 200 times as much biomass in fungi. Plants make up 80 percent of the world's biomass. And though there are many more bacteria than humans or plants, they account for only 13 percent of biomass because they are so tiny.

Outweighed

All the animals in the world make up only 0.44 percent of biomass, and insects account for half of that. Fish make up most of the rest. From the little bit that's left, livestock (farm animals) makes up a large proportion. Farm animals and pets make up nearly 92 percent of the biomass of all birds and mammals, leaving just over 8 percent for wild mammals and birds.

Your weight in carbon

Scientists often compare biomass by adding up the amount of carbon trapped in bodies of different types. That's not quite the same as the total mass of different types of organisms. While animals like humans are about 60 percent water (which doesn't count towards biomass), some plants are more than 90 percent water and a jellyfish is 95 percent water. So, while the biomass of humans is around half the biomass of jellyfish, the mass of jellyfish and their relatives is about 13 times the mass of whole humans.

DID YOU KNOW?

The biomass of jellyfish and their relatives is as great as that of all farmed animals.

36 Spiders and squid have blue blood

And they're not alone. So do octopi, crustaceans (like lobsters), and some mollusks (animals like slugs and snails).

Red, blue, green, violet...

Your blood is red because the chemical that carries oxygen in it, called hemoglobin, contains iron. When oxygen is attached to the iron, it makes iron oxide (the same as rust), which is red. Animals like squid and lobster have a different chemical in their blood to carry oxygen, called hemocyanin. In this, oxygen attaches to copper, making a blue compound. Red and blue aren't the only options. Some worms and leeches, and a lizard that lives in New Guinea, have green blood. And some marine (sea-living) worms have violet blood!

37 Your veins don't hold blue blood

If you have pale skin, you can probably see some of the veins carrying your blood under your skin and will have noticed they look blue. But if you cut yourself, your blood is always red. Some people assume blood is blue after it has given up its oxygen, but it's not—it's a darker red.

Thick skinned

Veins are under your skin, and skin absorbs all light except for blue light. This means the light reflected back from your veins is blue. The exact shade also depends on the thickness of the walls of the vein. Smaller veins have thinner, more translucent walls, which makes the blood look more red.

38 A cockroach can live without its head

It can survive up to three weeks, but after that it dies of starvation or dehydration (lack of water). There are other things besides eating and drinking that you do with your head, but a cockroach has different ways of managing those tasks!

Easy breaths

You breathe through your nose and mouth. Without a head you couldn't breathe, but some insects, like cockroaches and grasshoppers, breathe through holes in their body called "spiracles." These lead to tubes in the body where oxygen (O) is taken in and carbon dioxide (CO_2) is released back into the air. The cockroach doesn't use muscles to breathe—the air just flows in and out without the cockroach doing anything. This is called "passive breathing" and all insects do it.

Stop bleeding!

Many animals would bleed to death if they lost their head. A cockroach, though, doesn't have a heart pumping blood around its body at pressure as you do. Blood will leak slowly from the neck, but it will clot before the animal loses too much blood. Your blood clots, too—that's how scabs form. But a mammal can lose a lot of blood quickly because the heart keeps pumping it even if it's leaking out through a cut.

Aimless

A cockroach uses its eyes and antennae to find its way around and to locate food and water. Without a head, it doesn't have these, so it just wanders around aimlessly. Even if it found some food or water, it couldn't eat or drink without a head—and that's what kills it in the end (unless something else eats it first!)

39 A reindeer's eyes change from gold to blue in winter

Reindeer live in the Arctic, where the winters are cold and dark. There is little sunlight in the middle of winter, and therefore little light for reindeer to see by. The reindeer's eyes turn blue when structures inside the eye change to capture more light, enabling the reindeer to see better in low light.

Bright blue eyes

The retina is a layer at the back of the eye that contains the light-sensitive cells used to see. There are collagen fibers between the light-sensitive cells. In winter, pressure increases inside the reindeer's eye, pushing the fibers closer together. This makes bluer light reflect from the retina.

Golden eyes of summer

In summer, there is almost permanent daylight in the Arctic. Pressure reduces in the reindeer's eye, allowing the collagen fibers to spread out more and reflect more of the light that falls on the eye. Now the eyes look yellow or golden.

Human eyes can change, but it can only happen once

Reindeer eyes are the first known to change with the seasons. Your eyes stay the same in winter, summer, and all year round. What's more, your eyes are blue, green, or brown depending on how much of the pigment melanin there is in a different part of the eye, the iris. Many babies are born with blue eyes that change during the first year or two to become green or brown. This is because there isn't much melanin in the eyes when a baby is born, but it builds up over time.

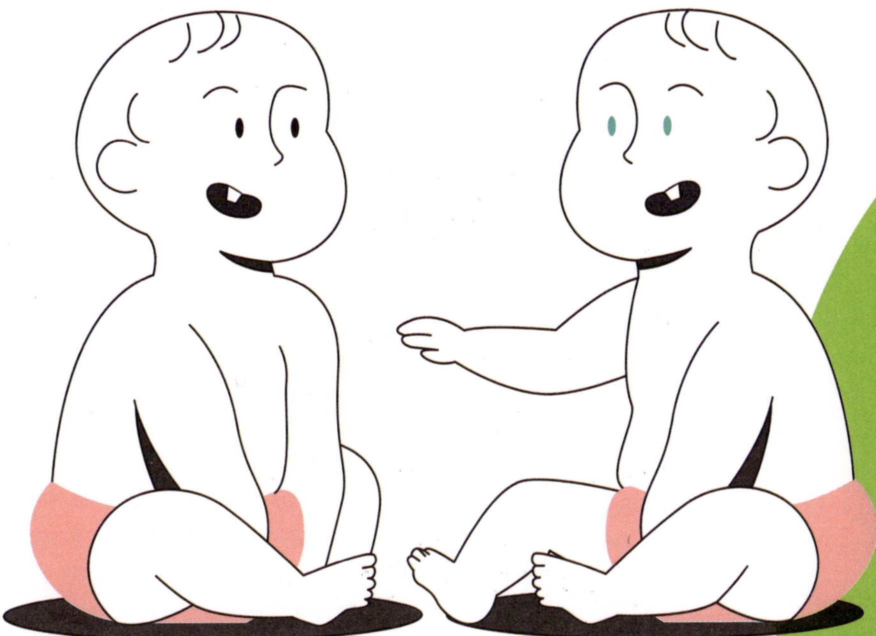

40 Tuna use sharks as back scratchers

Sharks have rough skin covered in tiny toothlike bumps called "denticles." If you stroke a shark in one direction (don't try it!), its skin feels smooth, but in the other direction it feels like sandpaper. Tuna mostly scrape themselves against the rear end of the shark, as far away from the shark's real teeth as possible. The scraping knocks parasites off the tuna.

Biting bugs

Parasites are organisms that live in or on another organism (the host) and feed from it. Parasites include tapeworms that live in the body of a larger animal, as well as lice and fleas that live on the skin of an animal. Plants like mistletoe that grow in trees and sink their roots into its bark are also parasites. Some parasites take the food the host eats, leaving less to nourish the host. Others feed on the host's blood (if the host is an animal) or sap (if it's a plant). Parasites, including worms, lice, and fleas, can live on humans.

Get off!

Getting rid of parasites is a problem for many animals. If an animal has too many parasites, it can die from lack of food or from blood loss. Some parasites also carry diseases that can infect and harm an animal or plant. Some mammals, such as monkeys, pick parasites off their friends and relatives. This grooming is helpful and creates strong social bonds between animals. Fish can't pick off parasites from themselves or each other as they have no limbs, but they can scrape against things.

41 Half your body isn't you

Your body is home to lots of microbes that are not part of you, but that are often essential to keep your body working properly.

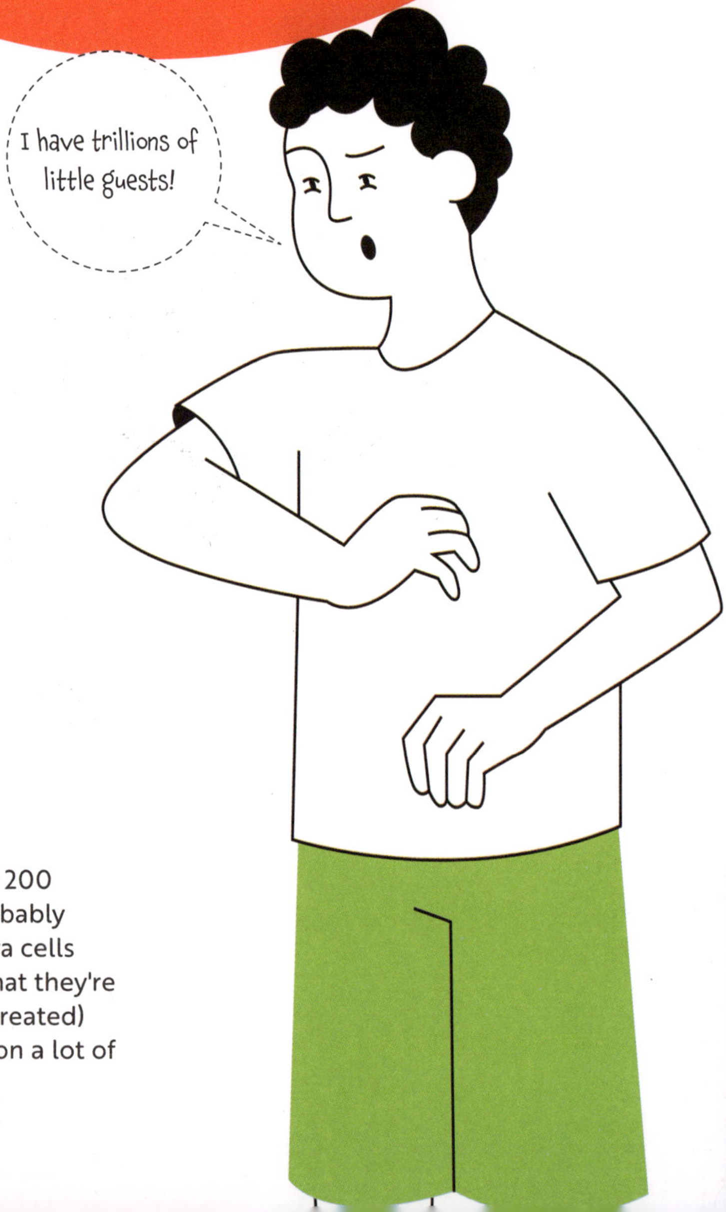

Cells everywhere

All living things are made up of cells. These are tiny self-contained units of different types. Your body has muscle cells, bone cells, skin cells, and many other types of cells. Some very small living things, called microbes, have only one cell (see page 37). Some of these are bacteria, which have very simple cells. Bacteria live everywhere—in the water, in the soil, and even in rock. And many live in other, larger, living bodies, including yours.

Trillions!

An adult human body has around 30 trillion cells—that's 30,000,000,000,000—of about 200 types. On top of that, there's probably around the same number of extra cells that aren't part of the body (in that they're not human cells your body has created) but that live in or on it. You rely on a lot of these for your body to function!

Bad bacteria, good bacteria

Some bacteria cause disease or infection. If you fall over and get a cut or graze, you should wash it to remove any bacteria that could cause infection. But not all bacteria are bad. Many don't affect us at all, and some are actually helpful! Bacteria in your gut help break down the food you eat. Without them, you couldn't digest your food properly. Lots of bacteria live on your skin, too. Your own personal collection of bacteria is called your "microbiome."

42 You can tell the temperature with a cricket

A cricket is a winged insect, rather like a grasshopper, with long rear legs. It makes a chirping sound that is easy to recognize on summer days. Amazingly, the speed at which a cricket chirps relates exactly to the temperature; its chirp changes as the day gets hotter or colder. If you know how to work it out, you can use a cricket as a thermometer.

Calculating with crickets

To work out the temperature from a cricket, you need to count how many times the cricket chirps in 14 seconds; then add 40 to that number. This gives you the temperature in degrees Fahrenheit. So, if the cricket chirps 35 times in 14 seconds, the temperature is about 75°F (24°C).

DID YOU KNOW?

Crickets have their ears on their front pair of legs. Compared to its total size, they are some of the smallest ears of any creature in the animal kingdom.

Here's the rub

Crickets make their chirping noise by rubbing their wings together. One wing has a "scraper" and the other has a "file." Rubbing one against another makes a sound like rubbing your thumbnail along a comb. The speed at which a cricket chirps is set by its muscles because it's moving its muscles to make the noise. The muscles move more easily when warm—just as you warm up before exercise to make your muscles work better and to prevent being injured. Most crickets that make a sound are male. They do it to attract a female, as well as to warn off competing male crickets.

43 Before you were born, you had a tail

It takes nine months for a human embryo to grow into a baby. It goes through a lot of changes in that time, turning from a small clump of cells into a functioning baby. Early on, it has a tail, but that slowly shrinks and is usually gone by the time the baby is born.

A tail inside

Humans have evolved from earlier mammals that had tails. The gene for growing a tail is still in our bodies, but we don't use it once we have developed beyond being an embryo. From 11 weeks' gestation (growth inside the mother), a human embryo is called a fetus. A fetus starts with a tail, but it shrinks—or rather, it doesn't grow—as the fetus gets larger. Instead, the tail becomes the tailbone, or coccyx, inside the body. It's at the base of the spine, just above your bum.

Outside tails

Just occasionally, a person is born with a bit of a tail, but it's not long enough to be useful like a monkey's tail.

You also had gills!

Further back in evolutionary history, all four-legged mammals evolved from fish-like animals that came out of the water to live on land. All fish have gills, and the gene for growing gills also still exists in mammalian bodies. Slits in the neck of an early embryo look like the gills that our very ancient ancestors used to breathe in water.

44 Bees are electric

Honeybee swarms produce more electricity than storm clouds or electric dust clouds. For the same volume, they make up to eight times as much electricity as a storm cloud and up to six times as much as an electric dust cloud. The denser the swarm of bees, the more electricity they generate: up to around 1,000 volts per cubic m (35 cubic ft) of bees.

Whizzing wings

Bees probably make static electricity accidentally, from the friction of moving their wings through the air, or they might produce the electricity deliberately for some purpose we don't know about. It is known that the hairs on bumblebees' bodies respond to electrical fields produced by flowers and that they use this sense to help them find food. Honeybees detect changing electric fields to help them communicate using the "waggle dance" they perform to share information about where to find flowers.

Another sense

Other animals are known to detect electrical fields using an extra sense that humans don't have. We use sight, hearing, smell, taste, and touch to discover information about the outside world. Animals, including sharks, dolphins, amphibians, some fish, and the monotremes platypus and echidna, detect the electricity produced by animals they want to eat. This sense is called "electroreception." It has evolved separately several times in different animals. Most of these animals detect electricity through water, whereas bees work with electricity transmitted through the air.

45 A starfish arm can grow a new starfish

Many people know that if a starfish loses an arm, it can grow a new one—but sometimes a starfish arm by itself can grow a new body and four more arms!

46 Some lizards can snap off their tail

They can deliberately drop their tail and run away if caught by a predator, and then they can grow a new tail. The new tail has only cartilage, and not bone, in the middle. And the old tail stays wriggling on the ground on its own to keep the predator busy!

Making new parts

All animal bodies have different types of cells. Humans have bone cells, skin cells, blood cells, and many other types of cell. When you were growing in your mother's womb, you began with cells that were all the same but that could become and produce cells of different types. These are called "stem cells." Later, you kept a few stem cells in special places in your body, such as inside your bones, but they aren't the right type to grow a new arm or a new eye.

A starfish has stem cells in the central part of its body that can grow a new arm. It can make all the different types of cells it needs and arrange them in the right way, in order to replace parts that are lost. If a starfish is cut in half, both halves can grow new arms. And as long as an arm has a chunk of the middle part still attached, it has the stem cells to grow a whole new starfish around itself!

47 A minced-up sea sponge can put itself back together

Sponges are sea-dwelling animals. If they get cut up into small pieces, they can reassemble into a new sponge if the pieces are left to settle!

Pretty simple

Sponges have a simple body with just a few different cell types. They don't have any complex structures like a brain, bones, heart, or lungs. Unlike you, they have no formal body plan. You have a head at the top, legs at the bottom, and arms to the side, and all your important body organs are in the middle. Your main sense organs—eyes, ears, mouth, and nose—are clustered on your head. A sponge has no separate head, arms, legs, body organs, or special sensory organs. It is often a cup shape or blob. It has two main types of cells and a jelly-like substance that fills the gaps between other cells and holds the sponge in shape. One type of cell has a "flagellum"—a movable thread that waves in the water. This makes water flow through the sponge, and the sponge absorbs food from the water. Because the sponge is so simple, it just needs to group its two types of cells properly, and it can put itself back together after a terrible accident. Bits of sponges broken off by stormy seas can regenerate, grow new cells, and start life as a new sponge.

48 Flatfish have both eyes on the same side of their body

Most animals have two matching halves, left and right, that are mirror images. But a flatfish has both eyes on the same side of its head and it often looks very different on its two sides.

Left and right, or top and bottom?

Flatfish live on the seabed. They are thin and flat, with eyes on the top and a mouth usually underneath. But the top and bottom were once left and right. The fish evolved from ancestors that swam upright in the water and with an eye on each side. They didn't flatten from the top; they just tipped over onto a side. It's no use having an eye that looks straight down into the sand (and it's probably not comfortable). The eye that was once on the side moved around to the top, putting both eyes on the same side of the fish.

Roving eye

Baby flatfish start off with an eye on each side like other fish. One eye gradually moves as the fish grows.

Radial symmetry

Bilateral symmetry

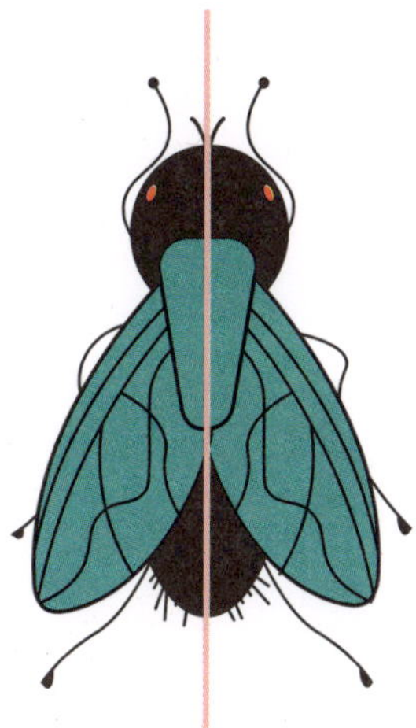

49 Starfish don't have left and right

Humans, and many other creatures, have an axis of symmetry that divides them in half vertically from top to bottom. The left side and the right side look identical. This is called "bilateral symmetry." But a few animals, including starfish and their relatives, have radial symmetry. This means a starfish is "made" by taking a portion—one arm and a chunk of the central body—and rotating it, copying the arm five or more times. A starfish has a top and bottom surface, but no left or right.

50 The oldest part of a tree is in the middle

Trees lay down a new layer each year, with the oldest part of the tree trunk being right in the middle. When a tree is cut down, we can tell how old it is by counting the "rings" inside. But while it's still alive, it's hard to tell exactly how old it is.

Recording history

The very central part of a tree is the part that grew as a sapling, sometimes hundreds, or even thousands, of years ago. You might have seen slices of old trees in a museum with labels that show what was happening in the world when each ring was laid down. A tree grows more quickly in warm summer weather and more slowly during the winter. The tree trunk shows light and dark stripes, or rings, and we can count either—but not both—to work out the age. The light stripes are wider and show spring and summer growth. The dark rings are thin and mark the time when growth slows down and stops for the winter.

Past worlds

Scientists can learn about the climate in the past by looking at tree rings. If there is a particularly dry year, a tree doesn't grow as well and adds only a thin ring. Trees grow best, and put down the thickest rings, when it is cool or warm (but not too hot or cold) and wet.

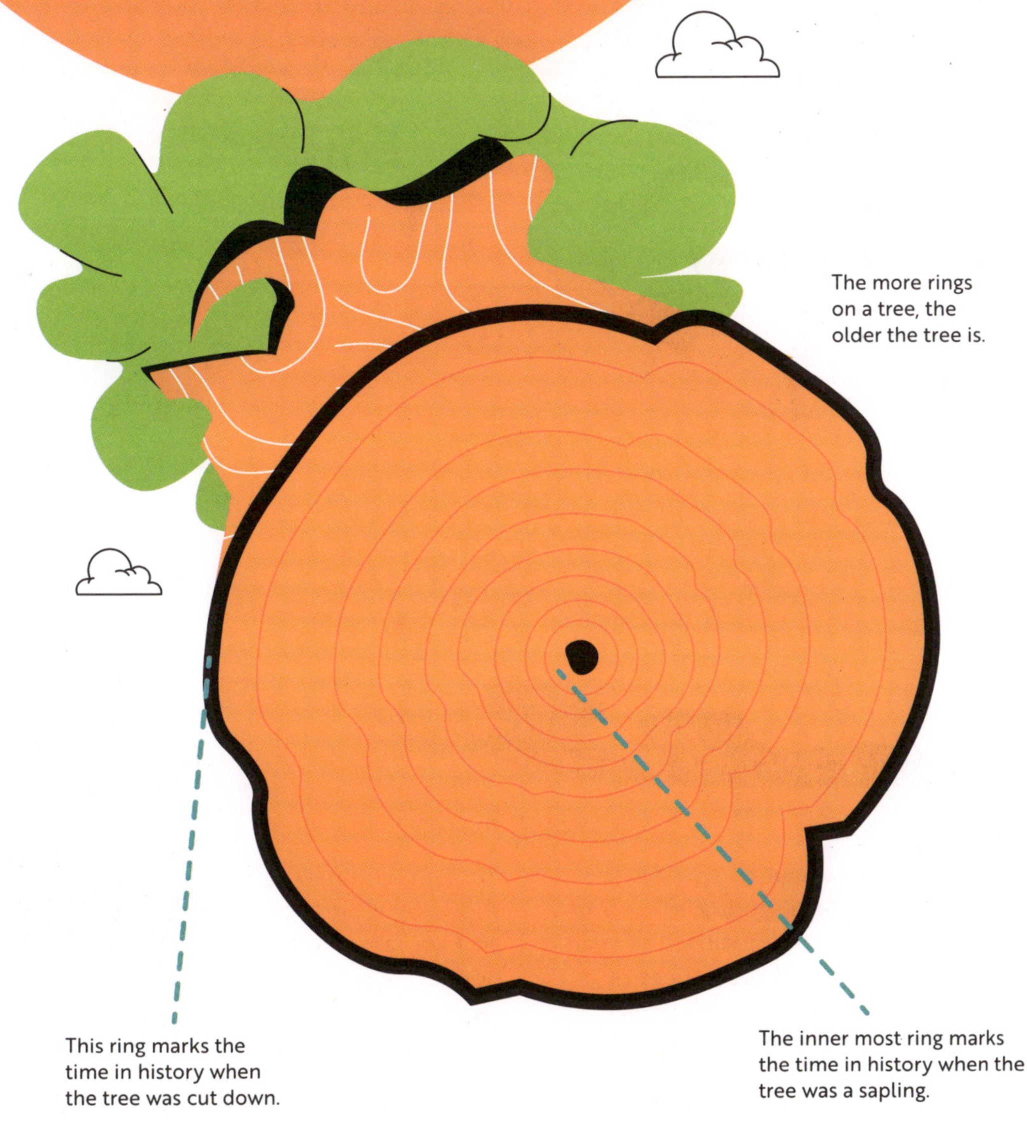

51 Lions are lazy a lot of the time...

...Or at least they look lazy to us. Lions tend to lie around resting and sleeping up to 21 hours a day. Are they lazy? Maybe, but their laziness is good for them.

Night and day

Lions live in areas where it's hot in the middle of the day. There's a lot of light, and not many places to hide. For a lion to go hunting for fast-moving animals like gazelles and wildebeest in the daytime would be quite foolish. There aren't many places the lion can hide to creep up on them, and it would have to do a lot of running in the hot sun to catch anything. The lion would use a lot of energy, wear itself out, and might not even catch a meal. Instead, lions hunt when it's cooler and the sky is darker. It's easier for lions to prowl around in the shadows, and they stay cooler while hunting.

Saving energy

Animals need to be careful with their energy. Humans are unusual in that they are usually able to get food whenever they need it, without going to much effort. For most animals, the energy they get from food is precious and hard to obtain. They can't afford to waste it by hunting at unsuitable times. It's far better to lounge around all day and just hunt in the cool evening when prey might not even see them coming.

52 Most of your body is new

Your body, like the bodies of all things, is made of cells. Most cells don't last very long. They wear out and must be replaced. Luckily, your body is good at generating new cells, which it does throughout your life. This means your body now contains little or none of the cells it contained when you were born—or even that it contained last year.

Making more

Cells make more cells by copying their own insides and then splitting into two. The new cells are exact copies of the original cells. Different types of cells reproduce to replace themselves at different speeds. The cells lining your gut have a hard life and only last two to three days. Your skin lasts longer, but you still get a completely new skin every two to three months. Your bone cells last about 10 years, so around a tenth of your skeleton is replaced each year. Your brain cells must last most of your life, though, so make sure to look after them!

Chemical engines

Your cells are tiny engines that carry out all the chemical tasks needed to keep your body going. Many are involved in storing and releasing the energy that you use to do things. Cells use chemicals from food, drink, and the air to keep your body going. One of the things they do is make new cells, both as you grow and to replace worn out or damaged cells.

53 Predators rarely eat other predators

You don't hear of lions eating cheetahs or crocodiles. They usually eat herbivores (animals that eat plants) rather than other carnivores (animals that eat meat). It's not because carnivores aren't tasty, though. It's partly because they might bite back, but it's mostly a result of how energy is produced and passed on through food.

Starting at Level 1

Scientists talk about "trophic levels," meaning levels of energy passed on in foods. The source of energy for all of us is ultimately sunlight. Plants use sunlight to build their leaves, roots, stalks, seeds, and fruit. They are Level 1 organisms, but they only convert about 10 percent of the energy they take from the Sun into potential food. Level 2 organisms are herbivores. They eat the plants, and then use the energy and chemicals they get from them to build their own bodies.

Congratulations—you have reached Level 3

Carnivores are Level 3 organisms. They eat the Level 2 herbivores. But again, the herbivores didn't put all the energy they got from food into growing. They spent a great deal of energy doing other things, including running around, keeping warm, reproducing, and just generally living. Only about 10 percent of their food energy is stored in their body and passed on to the carnivore that eats them. Carnivores also run around, reproduce, and keep warm. If another animal ate them, they are down to getting only 1/1,000th of the plant's original energy, and that's very inefficient.

54 All four-legged animals evolved from fish

Your ancient ancestors were fish that swam in the oceans 400 million years ago. In fact, you're more closely (or recently) related to a fish than to some land animals, such as slugs, scorpions, and insects.

All wet at first

Life on Earth probably evolved in the water, either in the sea or in pools on land. It began with tiny cells that exchanged chemicals with the water, and over billions of years led to complicated animals like fish, sea scorpions, and early relatives of squid. Until about 500 million years ago, Earth's atmosphere let in too much damaging radiation from the Sun for much to be able to live on land. Perhaps a few algae spread over the rocks, but everything else stayed in the water where it was safe.

New air, new animals

When the atmosphere changed, collecting a protective layer of the gas ozone, organisms could finally venture onto land. First came crustaceans—those with a hard, jointed outside like centipedes and scorpions. Then, around 400 million years ago, some fish strengthened their front fins until they could drag themselves around on these sturdy, stumpy "legs." These "fishapods" began to haul themselves up the beach onto the land and started to breathe air. They gave rise to amphibians, which spent time in and out of the water. From amphibians, reptiles evolved, and later came mammals and birds. All these had—and still have—the basic four-limbed body plan that the fishapods dragged from the sea.

55 A war was nearly fought over bird droppings

You'd think any fight about bird poop would be about getting rid of it, but this was about collecting it! Islands covered entirely in bird mess became a valuable resource in the 19th century because the droppings were used as fertilizer for crops.

From poo to food

In the 1850s, the Chincha Islands off the coast of Peru had no people, but it did have 60 million birds. These birds produced a lot of droppings and had been doing so for thousands of years. With little rain, the poop just piled up in vast heaps. The droppings, called "guano," were rich in nitrogen, which plants need to grow. When chemists discovered that adding nitrogen to soil makes crops produce more food, the hunt was on for sources of nitrogen. The Chincha Islands were suddenly very attractive and Spain seized them from Peru (they were reinstated to Peru in 1879).

DID YOU KNOW?

Half the nitrogen in your body has gone through the Haber process. Some has gone through a bird.

Nitrogen everywhere

Most of the atmosphere is nitrogen, so there's no real shortage of it. The problem is getting it from the air into plants. Some microbes in the soil "fix" nitrogen from the air into chemicals plants can use.

As populations around the world grew, so did the need for food. People became anxious about their food supply relying on bird poop found on small islands. Luckily, in the early 1900s, chemist Fritz Haber invented a way of taking nitrogen from the air to make a chemical to use in fertilizers. It means that food production today is four times more efficient than it was in 1900.

56 Crabs can make new anemones

The pom-pom crab grabs little anemones and clutches one in each claw to use as stinging weapons that it wields as it hunts for food. It can make more anemones as it needs them, forcing them to clone (copy) themselves.

Sharing is caring

If a pom-pom crab doesn't have an anemone, it will steal one from another crab. This leaves each crab with one claw empty, so they will both tear their single anemone in half and carry one half in each claw. The anemones can regenerate, so each half grows back into a whole anemone. Essentially, the crabs can farm the anemones they need, making them reproduce to supply the crabs' needs. Apart from being ripped in two, the anemones benefit from working with the crab. The crab drops bits of the food it catches with the anemones, and the anemones feed on the scraps that float around in the water.

Not the only weapon thieves

The violet blanket octopus tears the tentacles off deadly jellyfish and uses them to defend itself. A few other types of octopus carry a dead jellyfish around to use as a weapon. These octopi can't make their own poison, but they are quite capable of using the poison made by a jellyfish either to defend themselves or to sting animals they want to eat.

Eating poison

The poison dart frogs of South America go even further in stealing weapons they can't make for themselves. They eat poisonous insects and then store the poison in their own bodies. If another animal eats the frog, it's poisoned. Most other animals have learned not to eat them.

57 Arctic fish use antifreeze

If you live somewhere the weather often dips below freezing, you might know people who put antifreeze in their car to stop it freezing in winter. Antifreeze makes it difficult for bonds to form between water molecules to make ice. Fish that live in very cold seas in the Arctic have natural antifreeze to stop their bodies freezing.

Warm on the inside

Warm-blooded animals, including humans, control their body temperature using energy they take in from food. Cold-blooded animals, including fish, can't do this. On land, cold-blooded animals warm up by basking in the sun; they cool down by standing in a breeze or in the shade. Fish can only move to warmer or cooler areas of the sea, but there are no warm places in the Arctic. Antifreeze in their blood is their protection.

58 Chilled sea anemones live upside-down under the ice

A special type of white sea anemone lives on the underside of a shelf of ice that covers the sea in Antarctica. The anemone lives embedded in the ice with only its tentacles drooping down into the water.

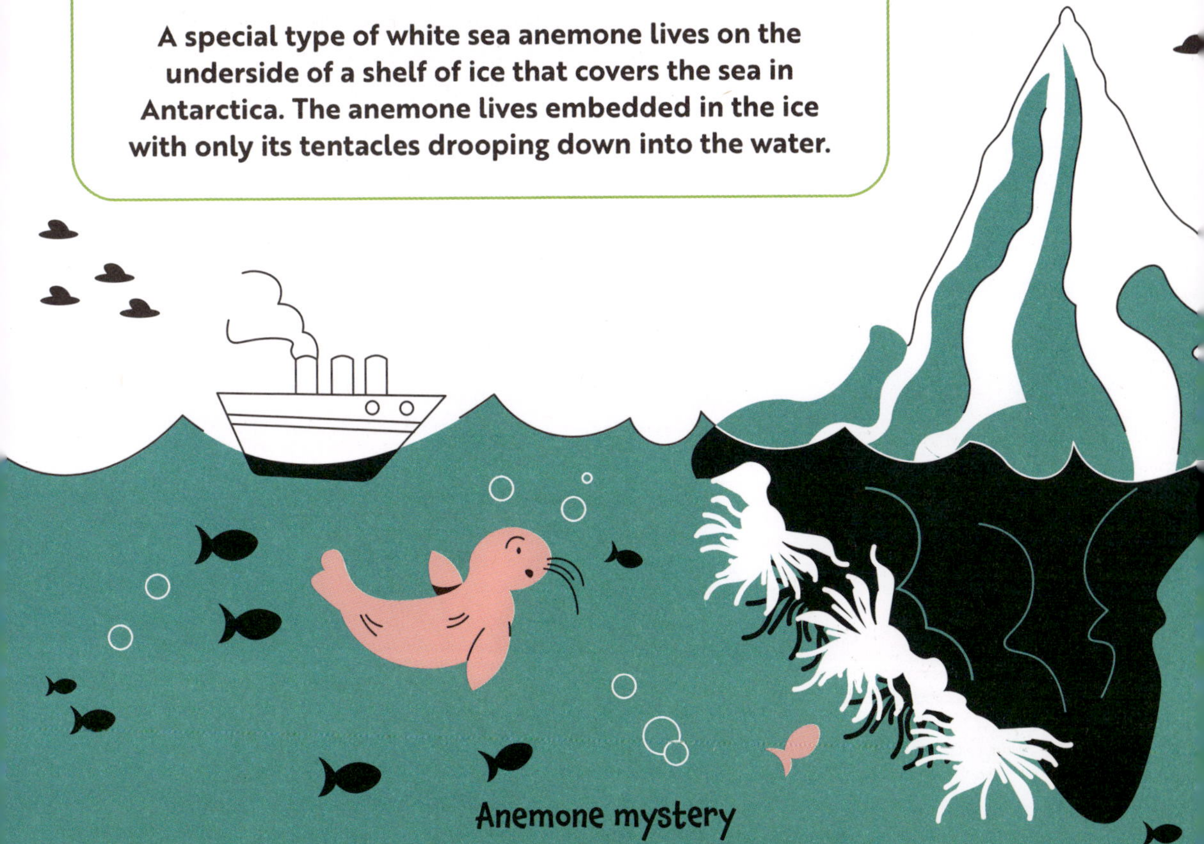

Anemone mystery

The scientists who discovered them couldn't work out how they survive without freezing or how they burrowed into the ice. Most anemones live the other way up, with their base fixed to a rock and their tentacles waving in the water above. The icy anemones not only live upside-down, but they manage to burrow into the ice, which should be too hard for them to wear away. They might make a chemical that dissolves the ice for them, but it's still a mystery to scientists.

59 The "mad hatterpillar" piles up its own old heads to look scary

Even the sound of it is scary! As caterpillars grow, they have to shed their outside and grow a new, larger one because their skin doesn't stretch as they get bigger. Along with their body skin, they shed their head covering. But instead of dropping it and walking away, gum-leaf skeletonizer caterpillars keep it on their head like a hat. They do it every time they molt, collecting a large pile of old heads. These rise up like a spike from the caterpillar's real head.

Two heads are better than one

Why would a caterpillar need extra heads? Experts think one reason might be to distract or confuse predators. A bird that usually picks up a caterpillar by the head might find a pile of heads a challenge. But there are worse things than being eaten by a bird. Some parasites lay eggs inside the heads of caterpillars. When the eggs hatch, the baby parasites munch on the living caterpillar. Having a tall pile of old heads as a hat might well protect against a parasite trying to lay an egg in the caterpillar's head.

Protective clothing

A pile of old heads is an odd way for a caterpillar to protect itself, but caterpillars do have dangerous lives. To protect themselves, some caterpillars grow long stinging hairs or spikes, and some are poisonous. Some have patterns that look like large eyes so that they appear to be an entirely different animal.

60 A sponge doesn't know what it looks like

A sponge is a very simple organism that lives in the sea. It can feed and reproduce (make more sponges), but it can't make noise, move around, or see. It can't even see itself and its family of nearby sponges. It's just one of many simple organisms that can't see.

Open your eyes

Until about 550 million years ago, nothing on Earth could see, because eyes had not yet evolved. Some organisms had simple "eye spots" that could tell light from shade, but they couldn't see a seaweed or a rock like you can. If you look at a picture or fossil of a very early animal, like Dickinsonia, you are seeing something that was never seen by anything else when it was alive.

Again and again

Eyes are so useful to animals that they have evolved again and again—probably 40 times or more. They started as a patch of light-sensitive cells clustered together. Over time, a pit in the animal's body formed, with the cells inside it. A thin protective skin formed over the opening to the pit, and this eventually evolved into a lens that could focus an image on the back of the eye pit. From there, an eyeball was just a few evolutionary steps away.

Now we see you...

The evolution of eyes changed life on Earth forever. Once animals could see each other, it became much easier to hunt for prey. And the hunted animals could see the predators coming, so they started to hide or disguise themselves so they were harder to spot.

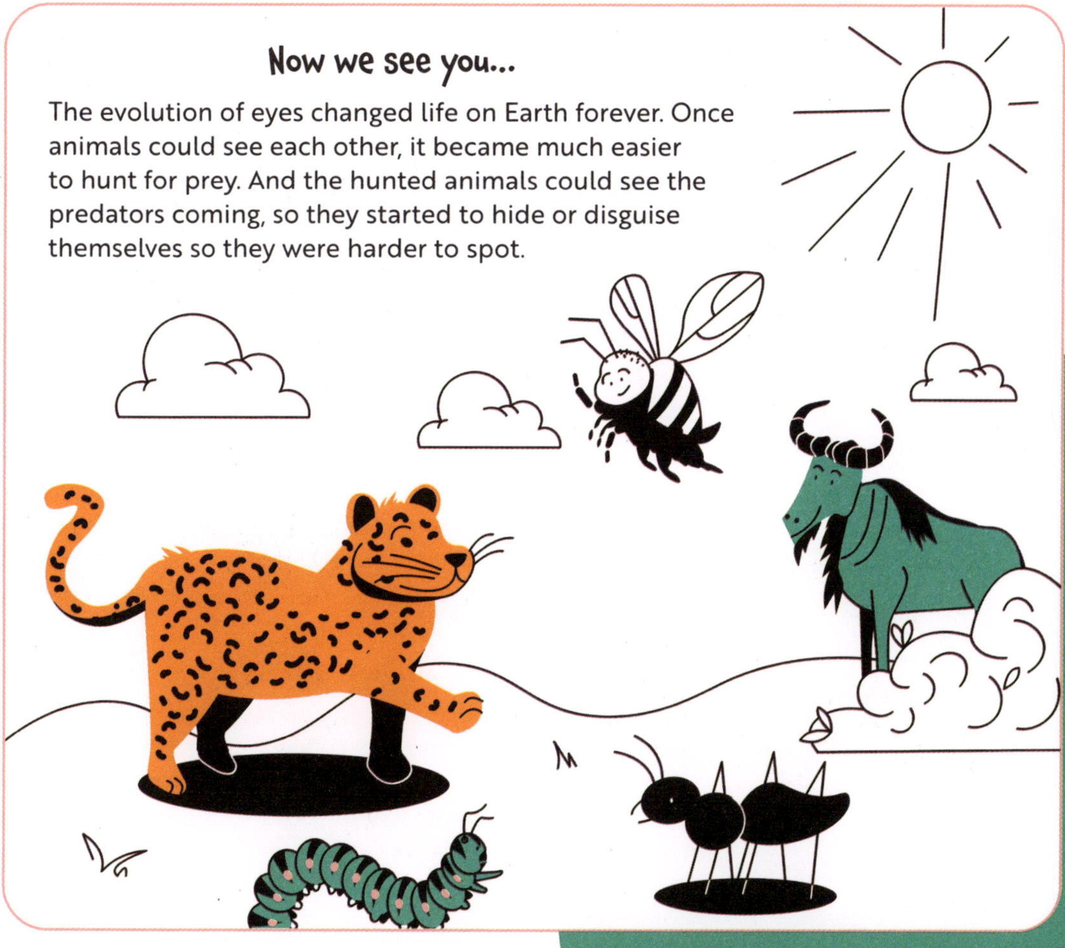

61 A submerged plane is a good home for coral

We're not talking about planes that are still flying, but old planes that have fallen or been dropped into the sea. Coral also grows on other objects with hard surfaces that are left lying in warm shallow seas.

Making a home

Coral polyps are tiny animals similar to sea anemones. They build a hard shell around themselves for protection and feed on particles drifting in sea water. New coral polyps settle and build a home on the shells of previous coral. Over hundreds of years, they build up huge coral reefs that are an important habitat for thousands of other species of sea creatures. Coral polyps rely on algae that live inside them and photosynthesize. Because the algae need sunlight, coral reefs grow in shallow seas.

Coral in danger

Climate change and irresponsible fishing practices destroy coral reefs. Hotter seas with a different mix of chemicals kill coral polyps and the algae that live in them. Boats dredging the seabed smash up coral reefs. If the reefs vanish, the other animals that also live on the reefs will have nowhere to live. We can help coral by encouraging new reefs.

Made to measure

While natural reefs take many years to build, coral can be coaxed into building on structures dropped into the sea just offshore. They will fix to the hard surface of a tank, car, statue, or almost anything else. They're not fussy homeowners! Coral can be grown in nurseries and then introduced to a new home on a submerged hard surface where they reproduce to make a new reef.

62 You're taller in the morning

If you're going to mark your height chart, you'll seem taller if you do it as soon as you get up. During the day, the weight of your head, and gravity dragging on your body, squashes the bones in your back closer together, making you shorter. Your spine relaxes back to its full length overnight when you're lying down.

Squashy and stiff

Your backbone consists of small individual bones called vertebra. Together, these bones form the vertebrae, or backbone. Each vertebra is separated by a round, flat cushion-like pad called an intervertebral disc. The discs protect the bones from grating and grinding together under pressure.

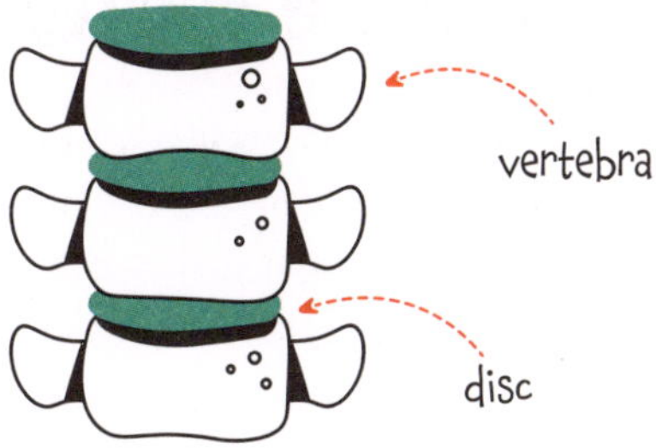

DID YOU KNOW?

Astronauts grow taller in space where gravity isn't compressing the spine.

Bendy backs

If your backbone was one solid bone, you wouldn't be able to bend. Having lots of small bones with gaps between means you can curve your back and neck. Some animals can curl it a lot more than we can. A swan's neck can curve a great deal, and a snake can make its body into wave shapes.

63 You have as many neck bones as a giraffe

Nearly all mammals have seven vertebrae in their necks. That includes you, mammals with shorter necks, and even giraffes with very long necks.

Big and bulky

A giraffe's seven cervical (neck) vertebrae are each much longer than yours. Because its neck is in only seven chunks, it can bend it up and down and side to side, but only within limits. It can't curl it.

64 Fish look down when they swim

Like other animals, we use vision to help us navigate (find our way), to avoid danger, and to find things we want, such as food or a safe place to shelter. Humans have a fairly easy time because we really only move in two dimensions of flat space and most things around us are standing still. But fish move in three dimensions—backward and forward, left and right, and up and down—and the water and everything in it is moving around them.

Where are you going?

A fish swimming in a river is surrounded by moving water and other things, such as plants, debris, and other fish, which are also moving. The water current tugs fish along, and they have to work against it to get where they want to go to. It's hard to navigate if nothing around you is keeping still. The only thing that doesn't move is the riverbed. How other things, including light and shadow, move relative to the riverbed tells the fish how to compensate for the movement to control where it's going. By looking down, fish can work out the speed and direction changes they need to make in order to go where they want. Why a fish is going somewhere and what it hopes to do when it gets there, is a question science hasn't explored yet.

65 There are more trees on Earth than stars in our galaxy, the Milky Way

There are probably 100–400 billion stars in the galaxy, but more than three trillion (3,000,000,000,000) trees on Earth. That's about 10 trees for each star!

Shrinking numbers

While three trillion is a lot of trees, humans cut down around 15 billion trees every year. Our ancient ancestors lived in a world with close to six trillion trees, but nearly half have been lost over the last 10,000 years. People cut down trees to clear land for farming and building, and to gain wood to use as fuel or for making things, including buildings and ships.

Hot and cold

Around a quarter of the world's trees are in cool forests in North America, Russia, and Scandinavia. These are high-density forests that contain lots of trees with skinny trunks packed into a small area. Nearly half of all trees are in tropical and sub-tropical forests. The trees are not as densely packed there, but the forests cover larger areas. We need all these trees. They support valuable ecosystems and provide the oxygen we breathe.

66 There are more microbes in a cup of soil than there are people on Earth

There are around a billion microbes in every teaspoon of soil across 10,000 different types. There are eight billion people on Earth, so a whole cup of soil contains more than enough microbes to match the human population.

Micro helpers

Microbes carry out all sorts of essential tasks in soil that keep life on Earth going. They break down waste matter and turn it into chemicals that plants can use. They clean water and protect plants from disease, and they both produce and consume different gases.

67 Plants give each other warnings!

You don't think of plants warning each other if a hungry caterpillar or insect is approaching, but it turns out they do! Plants might not be able to run away or shout out loud, but they have other ways of fighting off attackers and letting each other know about danger.

Shout out

When they are attacked, plants release a chemical that works like a warning shout to other plants. Nearby plants detect the chemical in the air, and change the taste of their leaves, persuading caterpillars and insects that they're not worth eating.

A matter of taste

Some plants can make their leaves so yucky that caterpillars start eating each other instead of eating the leaves! This helps the plants twice over—there are fewer caterpillars left to eat them, and those caterpillars eat fewer leaves because they're already full after eating their former friends.

68 Plants can "hear"

Plants don't have ears, but leaves are sensitive to tiny movements of the air that we hear as sound. They respond defensively to the sound of a caterpillar munching leaves! If researchers play a recording of a caterpillar munching on leaves, the plants that "hear" it start making their leaves taste yucky.

DID YOU KNOW?

Some experiments have shown that plants grow better if they are talked to or if people play music to them—scientists are still trying to find out why.

69 Trees can taste deer saliva

When deer bite the branches of some types of tree, the tree sends chemicals to the leaves to make them taste bad, just as some plants do when attacked by caterpillars. But if a person breaks a branch, the tree doesn't change the taste of the leaves, it just sends chemicals to start fixing the wound. It seems the tree can "taste" deer saliva and act to protect itself—it's not just responding to the damage to its branch.

Bring on the wasps!

Elms and pines attacked by caterpillars that eat leaves have a vicious way of defending themselves. They produce chemicals that attract parasitic wasps that prey on the caterpillars. This doesn't necessarily mean that the tree can tell exactly what type of caterpillar is attacking it. It might be that the parasitic wasps recognize the chemical the tree releases when it's attacked and links this with the presence of caterpillars. But either the tree or the wasp is doing some clever chemical work!

70 Giraffes can thwart "talking" trees

Giraffes seem to know that trees warn each other about coming danger by releasing chemicals into the air when they are attacked by herbivores. Giraffes approach trees from downwind, so chemicals released by trees that have already been nibbled are blown away from the next tree-victim, not toward it. Without the warning from trees that have already been bitten, the next trees don't know they need to make their leaves taste bad. The result is that by sneaking up on the trees, the giraffes get to enjoy their lunch.

71 Zombie ants are controlled by parasites

If you get a parasite, such as a tapeworm or head lice, it's annoying, but it won't turn you into a zombie. Ants aren't as lucky. They are targeted by parasitic fungi that grow inside them, feeding on non-essential parts of the ant's body. But when it's time for the fungus to reproduce, that marks the end for the ant.

The fungus controls the ant's muscles, making the ant climb up a plant and attach itself there firmly. Then the fungus destroys the ant's brain, and a mushroom grows out of its head! The mushroom spreads the fungus spores into the wind, ready for the cycle to begin again.

72 Worms make ants look like berries

A type of nematode worm changes the body of its ant host to make it look like a tasty berry. The nematode changes the body of the ant, which is usually black, to bright red. The ant moves more slowly (probably because it's full of worms), holds its abdomen up away from its legs, and its abdomen becomes easy to break off. Birds snap up the ant bodies, mistaking them for berries. The nematodes inside the body are passed out in the bird's droppings, and when new ants take the droppings to feed ant larvae in their nest, the larvae become infected with the parasites. The nematodes grow and reproduce in the ant's body as it grows until that ant, too, comes to look like a ripe berry.

73 Some bacteria are big enough to see

Most bacteria are tiny—too small to see without a microscope. But one type, first found in the gut of a fish, is the size of a grain of salt. That doesn't sound big, but it is huge for a bacterium. It has about 2,000 times the volume of an average bacterium. Using humans as a comparison, this means that you would be about 12 times taller and 12 times wider than an average-sized person.

Going wrinkly

Bacteria don't eat, drink, or breathe. To get the chemicals they need from their environment, they absorb them through their outside "skin." But when any organism grows larger, the ratio of its volume (its insides) to its surface area (the total area of its outside) increases quickly. That means there is far less outside area for each cubic unit of inside volume. This makes it increasingly difficult for enough chemicals to enter (and leave) the cell through its surface. The big, fat bacterium gets around this by developing a wrinkly outside, which increases its surface area.

A common trick

Larger organisms, including humans, use the same trick to increase surface area. Your brain has a very convoluted surface, and the inside of your gut has lots of little bobbles all over the surface. Your lungs are divided into many small branches, too. Your brain does its important work at the surface, so having more surface area means you can be smarter. Your lungs absorb gases and your gut absorbs chemicals from food, so increasing the surface area helps you get more useful chemicals into your body.

74

Birds are magnetic...

...though only slightly. Lots of birds can detect Earth's magnetic field and they probably use it to navigate, especially birds that migrate (move seasonally). Some migratory birds have magnetite, a material containing iron, in the upper half of the beak, which might give them a magnetic sense that enables them to use Earth's natural magnetism. Alternatively—or as well—chemicals in their eyes might respond to magnetism and radiation.

Line up!

Migrating birds aren't the only animals that seem to use Earth's magnetic field. Trout also have magnetite in their noses. Fish such as sharks and stingrays respond to electrical fields to help find prey and avoid predators, and the organs they use for this might also detect magnetic fields that help them navigate. Other animals, including bats, turtles, fruit flies, bees, and even sea slugs, respond to magnetic fields. One type of giant sea slug turns its body east or north just before a full moon, suggesting it can tell not only where Earth's magnetic field is but the phase of the Moon!

Magnetic bacteria

Some bacteria contain enough magnetic material to line up along a magnetic field. This is not a response like that of animals, but rather a direct result of the bacteria being high in iron—they are simply magnetic. Some animals might have magnetic bacteria in their bodies, which can help them detect a magnetic field.

75 Ants make good farmers

Humans aren't the only species that farm animals and plants for food. Many ant species also farm plants, animals, or fungi.

High in the trees

Some ants plant the seeds of plants called "epiphytes" in cracks in tree bark and look after the seedlings as they grow. Epiphytes are plants that grow in trees, feeding off the tree. Ants sometimes fertilize their farmed plants with their droppings. Some types of ant feed on nectar (sweet liquid) from the plants, and some use the plants for shelter and protection.

Ant and aphid

Some species of ant farm aphids (greenfly). The aphids make honeydew the ants like to eat. The ants look after the aphids, protecting them from predators and sheltering their eggs in winter. They stroke the aphids to "milk" them of their honeydew.

Farming fungus

Ants have only farmed plants for 1–3 million years, but they've been farming fungus for around 60 million years. Leaf-cutter ants in South America cut out pieces of leaf and carry them to an underground farm where they "feed" them to the ants' fungus garden. The ants then eat the fungi—they never eat the leaves.

Special breeds

Just like human farmers, ants have changed the organisms they farm. The fungi in ants' fungus gardens aren't found anywhere else. The garden is cut off from the outside world, so there's no cross-fertilization with other fungi. And when an ant goes off to start a new colony, she takes a bit of the all-important fungus with her to begin farming.

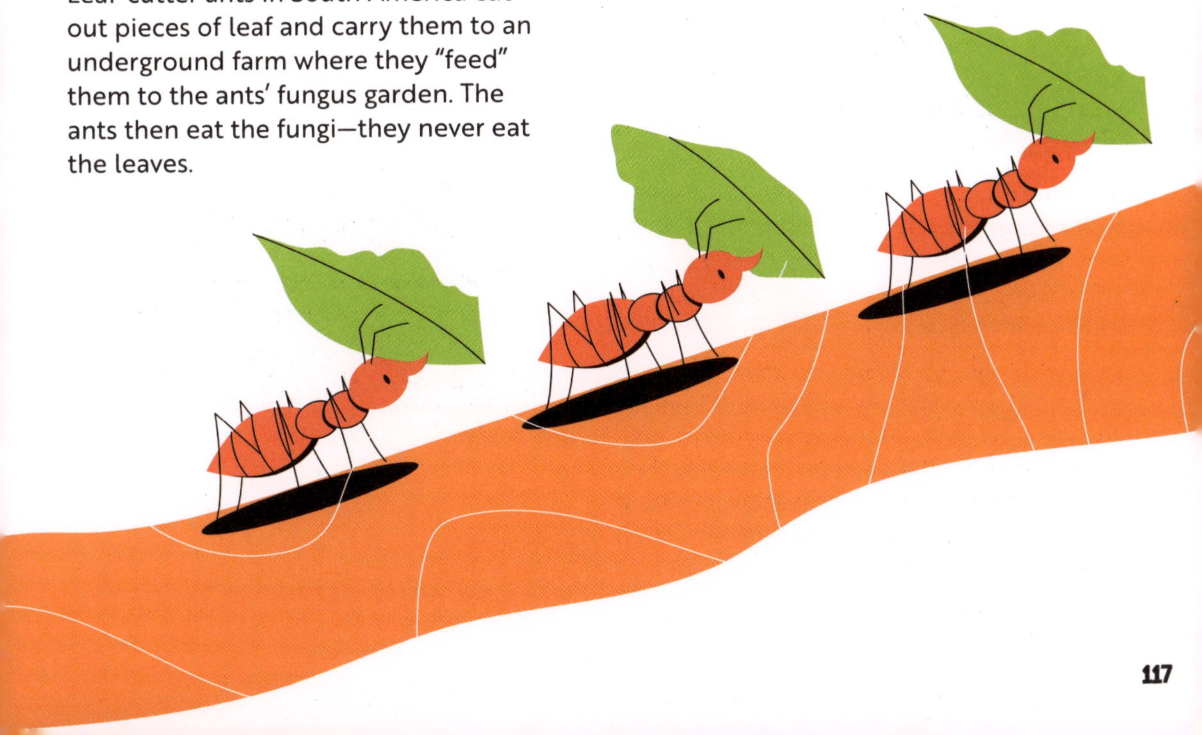

76 Green parrots aren't green

A green parrot contains no green pigments (chemicals that give a substance color). Parrot feathers have pigments only for yellow and red.

Bright and beautiful

Color in bird feathers is produced in three different ways—the feathers contain pigments; the feathers contain melanin, which makes them darker; or the structure of the feathers reflects light of different colors, which is the case for blue parrots. The structure makes any red and yellow light on the parrot cancel out, and reinforces the blue light instead. This is why our eyes see it as blue. A green parrot, which also has this feather structure, has some yellow pigment. Because blue and yellow make green when they are combined, the blue-feathered parrot looks green!

DID YOU KNOW?

Parrots have their own pigments not found in any other animal. These are called "psittacofulvins."

77 Flamingos are born gray

Like many other birds, flamingos gain pigments from their food. Flamingo chicks come out of the egg gray when they are born, but they become pink when they start to eat normal flamingo foods, such as shrimp and algae.

No pink food

Shrimp are colorless when living and algae are blue-green. When flamingos eat shrimp or algae, its liver breaks down chemicals, called carotenoids, in these food sources; the process makes red and orange pigments. The pigments collect in the feathers and produce shades of pink, when the flamingos eat shrimp. The feathers appear darker red-pink when the flamingos eat algae.

78 252 million years ago, nearly everything on Earth died

There have been five "mass extinction" events on Earth when lifeforms have gone extinct (died out). In the most catastrophic, which was 252 million years ago, more than 90 percent of species died out over the span of 20,000 years. Scientists call this event the "Great Dying."

Goodbye to all that

In the seas, 95 percent of all species died. On land, nothing larger than the size of a dog survived. Many plants and insects, which usually survive mass extinctions, fell victim. Earth was desolate, and it took millions of years for life to recover and repopulate the world.

Many ways to go extinct

Extinction events follow catastrophic climate change, which can itself have different causes. The Great Dying was probably caused by huge volcanic eruptions that lasted two million years, flooding Siberia in northern Russia with enough lava to cover the USA to a depth of several miles. Ash and dust poured into the sky, blocking the sunlight, so the temperature plunged; it killed plants, and all the animals died of starvation. After the ash and dust settled, the gases released by volcanoes then warmed the planet, raising the temperature and sea level beyond anything humans have ever seen. At the equator, the seawater was as hot as bathwater, at 40°C (104°F).

Dinosaurs were killed by an object from space

The extinction event that killed the last non-bird dinosaurs 66 million years ago happened when an asteroid (space rock) or comet crashed into Earth off the coast of Mexico. The impact caused clouds of rock and dust, and smoke blocked sunlight for months. High levels of carbon dioxide in the air led to the extinction of plants and animals, as well as global heating.

79 The toughest animal is a tardigrade

A tardigrade is a tiny micro-animal, at just 0.5 mm (0.020 in) long. Although it's small, it can survive in terrible living conditions. It's one of the creatures most likely to survive any kind of environmental catastrophe.

Tardigrades have a hard outside called a "cuticle," which means water doesn't evaporate from their bodies. They can survive extreme cold, well below freezing point, and even survive boiling water. They can go up to 30 years without food and can survive pressures six times that at the bottom of the ocean. Animals that live in extreme conditions are called "extremophiles." Tardigrades are the most extreme extremophiles! They've survived trips into space and blasts of radiation.

Shutting down

In bad times, a tardigrade can squeeze almost all the water out of its body and curl into a tiny ball. It then waits out the worst conditions, reducing its activity to less than 1/10,000th of its normal level. When conditions improve, it uncurls, rehydrates, and carries on its normal life.

Long ago

Tardigrades need a covering of water for normal activity, but they can live anywhere. Some live in the sea, but many live in moss and lichen in damp places on land—and they can survive in sand dunes and on the ice of Antarctica. They probably evolved around 500 million years ago and have survived all major mass extinctions, including the asteroid crash that wiped out the dinosaurs and the "Great Dying."

80 A deep-sea snail is covered in tiny chimneys

The bizarre snails have protective plates over their squashy parts that carry waste away from the snail's body. The snails are sometimes called "sea pangolins" because their plated bits look like the land-living pangolin.

Undesirable living space

In deep-sea vents, poisonous and scalding hot water up to 300°C (572°F) pours from under the seabed. Not much lives in these vents, so there isn't much to eat. The hardy sea-pangolin keeps a pouch full of bacteria that take chemicals from the seawater and produce food for the snail, so it doesn't need to find its own food. But the bacteria produce sulfur, which is poisonous to the snail. The snail combining this sulfur with other chemicals to make its scales, locking the sulfur away safely so that it can't harm the snail.

81 The strangest plant is *Welwitschia*

A desert plant that lives up to 2,000 years and can grow to 8.5 m (28 ft) sprawling over the ground has only two leaves.

A nice niche

Some organisms evolve strange structures or ways of life suited to very particular living conditions or places. These are called "ecological niches." *Welwitschia* is one such example that is adapted to the hot, dry conditions of the Namib desert in Namibia and Angola. Its taproot (the main root) goes deep into the ground to reach buried water, but the plant relies mostly on water collected as dew and fog. To collect more dew the leaves need to increase their surface area and so they grow larger—they can grow as long as 4 m (13 ft). The largest plants grow where there is the smallest amount of rain. The two leaves become tattered over years of exposure to hot sun, wind, and sandstorms, but they still collect water. Its tricks have worked—it has survived since the time of the dinosaurs.

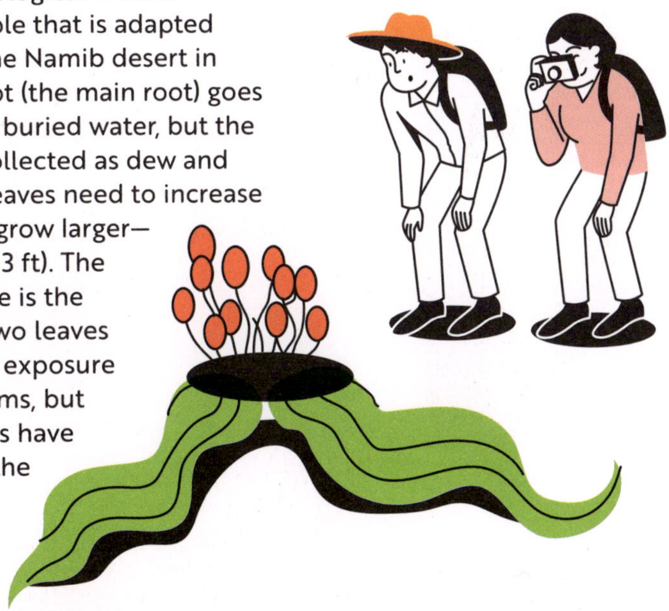

Glossary

Algae (singular, alga): Simple organism that photosynthesizes and usually lives in water.

Amphibian: Type of animal that must stay damp and lays its eggs in water. The young have gills and live in the water, but they change to live on land and breathe in air as adults.

Anemone: Squishy animal that lives in the sea. It attaches to rocks and waves its tentacles in the water to trap particles of food.

Artery: Blood vessel that carries blood away from the heart.

Atmosphere: The layer of gas surrounding a planet or moon.

Bacteria (singular, bacterium): A very simple single-celled organism.

Biomass: The mass of carbon in living things.

Cell: Small component of all living bodies. Cells are the building blocks of life; all organisms have at least one cell.

Cnidarian: Animal like a jellyfish that has a gelatinous jelly-like body and uses stinging cells to catch prey.

Collagen: Type of protein that forms the structure of living bodies. It can be stiff or bendy.

Crustacean: Type of animal with a hard outside and a jointed body. Many crustaceans live in water.

Digestion: The process of breaking down food in the gut and absorbing nutrients (useful chemicals) from it.

Dogfish: Small type of shark.

Evaporate: To turn to vapor through being heated.

Evolution: The process by which organisms change over long periods of time. As living conditions for an organism change, individuals that are best adapted to the new conditions thrive and reproduce. The more suitable features become increasingly common, until they become usual in that type of organism.

Fertilizer: Chemical that encourages plants to grow better.

Fluke: The lobes on the tail of a whale or dolphin.

Friction: Force produced by surfaces or objects rubbing against each other.

Fungus: Type of living thing, like a mushroom, that is neither plant nor animal and reproduces by spreading spores.

Gills: Organs on the side of a fish or immature amphibian that allows the animal to take oxygen from water.

Herbivore: Animal that eats plants.

Intervertebral disc: Soft cushion-like disc between each backbone vertebra that prevents the bones from grinding against each other.

Mature: To grow up and become an adult.

Microbe: Tiny single-celled organism.

Monotreme: Mammal that lays eggs. There are only five types of monotremata.

Navigate: To find the route to somewhere.

Nectar: Sweet, sugary liquid produced by flowering plants.

Organ: Structure in the body of an animal or plant that carries out a particular function, such as a heart pumping blood.

Organism: A living thing.

Parasite: Organism that lives in or on another living organism, using it for food, shelter, or other benefits.

Photosynthesis: The process by which plants, algae, and some bacteria use the energy from sunlight to make sugar and oxygen from water and carbon dioxide.

Phytoplankton: Photosynthesizing microorganisms of many types that live in the sea.

Pigment: Chemical that gives a plant, animal, or object its color.

Pitch: The high or low tone of a sound.

Polyp: Form of cnidarian with a cylindrical, jelly-like body and tentacles. Jellyfish are polyps only when young; coral and anemones keep the polyp form as adults.

Predator: Animal that hunts and eats other animals.

Radiation: Energy that moves through space as waves. The size of the waves (wavelength) sets what type of energy it is, including radio waves, light, and X-rays.

Reaction: How two or more chemicals change when put together. Atoms can be rearranged, breaking down substances and making new substances.

Remnant: Left-over piece of something.

Sapling: Young tree.

Spore: Reproductive cell of a fungus that works in the same way as a seed or fertilized egg to start growing a new organism.

Static electricity: Electric charge that builds up on a surface. If you rub an inflated balloon on your sweater, an electric charge builds up on the balloon.

Taproot: Main root of a primary root system that grows vertically down into the ground.

Ultraviolet: Radiation that has a slightly shorter wavelength than visible light.

Vein: Blood vessel that carries blood back to the heart from the body or lungs.

Vertebrae: Collection of bones that make up the backbone.

Index